Understanding the Industrial Revolution

Understanding the Industrial Revolution is a fresh, new exploration of this economic phenomenon of major importance. It describes theories of economic growth, shows how these can be applied to the revolution, and discusses them in the light of modern research. Furthermore it places the debate surrounding the social effects of industrialisation into the context of economic change during the period. This book includes discussion of:

- theories on the supply of capital, role of labour, and on demand
- innovation and entrepreneurship
- the significance of transport
- the impact of industrialisation on living standards

Each aspect of the Industrial Revolution in Britain is discussed in depth, focusing on the important debates and reviewing the most recent research.

Charles More is Principal Lecturer in History at Cheltenham and Gloucester College of Higher Education. His previous books include *The Industrial Age: Economy and Society in Britain 1750–1990* (2nd edition, Longman, 1997). He is a Fellow of the Royal Historical Society.

Understanding the Industrial Revolution

Charles More

London and New York

First published 2000
by Routledge
2 Park Square, Milton Park, Abingdon, Oxon, OX14 4RN

Simultaneously published in the USA and Canada
by Routledge
270 Madison Ave, New York NY 10016

Routledge is an imprint of the Taylor & Francis Group

Transferred to Digital Printing 2006

© 2000 Charles More

Typeset in Sabon by
Bookcraft Ltd, Stroud, Gloucestershire

British Library Cataloguing in Publication Data
A catalogue record for this book is available from the
British Library

Library of Congress Cataloging in Publication Data
More, Charles.
Understanding the industrial revolution / Charles More.
p. cm.
Includes bibliographical references and index.
ISBN 0-415-18405-5 (hbk) – ISBN 0-415-18405-3 (pbk)
1. Industrial revolution. 2. Industrial revolution–Great
Britain. I. Title
HD2321 .M575 2000
330.941'08–dc21   00-028065

ISBN 0-415-18404-5 (hbk)
ISBN 0-415-18405-3 (pbk)

Printed and bound by CPI Antony Rowe, Eastbourne

Contents

Figures

Tables

Preface

This book is designed to make the Industrial Revolution more comprehensible to students and non-economic historians. I hope that it will enable those who read it to understand the economic reasoning behind different explanations even if their knowledge of economics is limited.

After a brief introduction which sets out the scale of industrialisation in Britain between 1750 and 1850, Chapter 1 starts with a section on land, labour, capital and productivity which can be skipped by anyone with more than basic economics. Next, it outlines models – simplified representations of economic processes – of the Industrial Revolution. The succeeding chapters review these in more depth and compare their explanations of industrialisation with the fruits of historical research. This approach was influenced by Peter Gatrell's *The Tsarist Economy*. I read this a few years ago and was struck by the way its treatment illuminated the economic past, which often seems a mass of unrelated facts and theories.

The book is focused entirely on industrialisation – its causes and immediate economic impacts. It is not a complete economic history of the period, a number of which are listed in the bibliography to the Introduction, and so there are several omissions. Agriculture is not treated in detail. It was very important, and Chapters 7 and 8 make it clear why; but a detailed account of agricultural change does not in itself explain industrialisation. There is uneven coverage of the period of the book, with more attention paid to the earlier part because that was when rapid industrial growth began. Its continuation is important but this book's main concern is why it started, so canals and roads are discussed in more detail than railways, and so on. But the effects of industrialisation on living standards were long-term and so for this subject a discussion of the whole period up to 1850 is pertinent. There is another reason for the choice of 1750–1850: by setting wide limits to the period of the Industrial Revolution, it avoids assigning specific dates which then require justification. Economic phenomena were rarely confined within particular dates, even though statistical measurement demands definite beginnings and ends, and it seems best to avoid long-winded argument about dating when precision is not possible. Finally, Ireland is omitted as it experienced only limited industrialisation; its economic development was in most respects completely different to Great Britain's. So far as statistics are available which distinguish Great Britain from the whole United Kingdom of Great Britain and Ireland, as it was from 1801, I have used them.

Note that the tables, from which the data is drawn for many of the figures, appear at the end of the relevant chapter.

The following abbreviations for the most important journal titles in the field of economic history are used throughout the book:

EcHR   *Economic History Review*
JEH   *Journal of Economic History*

I am indebted to Bernard Alford for his careful reading of the text and his perceptive suggestions, and am also very grateful to Peter Wardley for discussion and advice, and an anonymous reader for valuable comments. I would also like to thank my wife Hilary for her support.

The scope of the Industrial Revolution

Revolution implies suddenness, as with the American and French revolutions which lasted a few years; but the Industrial Revolution was not a sudden event. However, other phenomena have been described as revolutions while occurring over a long period of time. The Scientific Revolution of the sixteenth and seventeenth centuries is a case in point. The fact is that the phrase 'Industrial Revolution' is now so ingrained that there is no point in trying to jettison it. What is important is to establish the different ways in which historians have conceptualised the 'revolutionary' nature of the changes.

Some have seen 'revolution' as shorthand for large-scale structural change in the economy; such a dramatic word is used to highlight the extent of the changes. In this view, the Industrial Revolution was a continuation of earlier change; it was not different in kind but merely in degree. Therefore its causes were not novel but rooted in the past, and the agenda for historical research is to chart the progress and exact nature of the changes. To others, however, the Revolution constituted a complete shift in the process of economic growth: it was this which was revolutionary. According to this interpretation, before the eighteenth century there was no mechanism by which long-term sustainable growth could take place. By the mid-nineteenth century such growth was an established fact of life: for the first time rapid population increase was accompanied by sustained growth in income per person. The revolution lay not in the speed, but in the shift from a hitherto inevitable correlation between increasing population and declining income per person. The most important thing, for these historians, is to discover why the changes occurred, and why they occurred in this particular period.

Historians – and economists – have therefore tended to explain the Industrial Revolution in different ways. Some have focused on the long-term nature of economic growth in Europe, seeing British industrialisation as one, striking, part of this. Others, particularly economists, have formulated general propositions about economic growth: to them the Industrial Revolution is one instance of such growth, albeit a very important one. And some have seen the Industrial Revolution as a dramatic, once and for all, change.

Needless to say, with such a diffuse phenomenon there has been frequent debate about when it occurred. The French Revolution can be safely assigned to a few specific years, although, of course, its causes may have lain decades earlier and its aftermath still be with us today. The Industrial Revolution is much more difficult to date. No one supposes that individual years have a particular significance: decadal turning points are usually taken for dating purposes, but this is purely for convenience. Few historians would go back much before 1750, although some trace causal factors back for centuries. Many prefer later dates: 1760 is often mentioned, in part because a number of important inventions appeared soon afterwards; 1780 also has followers. Some point out that the absolute impact of industrialisation only became widespread in the nineteenth century. Terminal dates are even more difficult: 1830 is popular, partly because steam railways, which had only just appeared, first became widespread in that decade. Railways can be seen as marking the beginning of a new stage of maturity, or as the end of the heroic period of the Industrial Revolution. In the first case 1830 is a logical end point, in the latter case 1850, by which time most of the main railways had been built. Statistically, although there is much debate, there does seem to be a growing consensus that the rate of growth of industrial production accelerated sharply between 1760 and 1780, and continued to grow more slowly thereafter, reaching a peak of 3.5 per cent per annum around the 1830s; so dating by statistics does not lead to firmer conclusions than other methods.

The years 1750–1850 have been chosen here not because the author considers them magical turning points but for precisely the opposite reason. Choosing a fairly expansive period avoids having to justify particular dates as 'turning points'. 1750 and 1850 are chronological conveniences, although in the Conclusion it is suggested that they might be as good as any other dates as markers for the beginning and end of the whole phenomenon.

Industrialisation and its measurement

Industrial Revolution implies industrialisation – that is, both the absolute growth of industry, and its expansion relative to the other sectors of the economy, those being agriculture and services. 'Industry' in this context covers manufacturing, mining and building, known as sub-sectors.

Not surprisingly, the production increases for industries such as cotton and iron, which are always associated with the Industrial Revolution, are far higher than for other industries: output rose by one hundredfold or more. But practically all industries increased their output substantially, even old, established ones such as glass-making (see Table I.2).

The output of agriculture and services also expanded in this period. This broad-based expansion does not always occur during industrialisation. By the late nineteenth century, for instance, Britain was still industrialising but agricultural output was actually falling. The increase in service output is more predictable. The growth of some services might be positively necessary for industrial growth; transport is an example. In the case of other services, such as retailing, higher incomes will lead to greater expenditure on them. The growth of services was also associated with the rapid urbanisation which took place at the same time as, and was in part caused by, industrialisation. Service output is usually assumed to have grown at about the same rate as the economy as a whole, although statistical indicators for it are very uncertain.

Finally, there was a growth in income per person across the economy. Although the figures, which are discussed further in the Appendix, are very uncertain, it seems likely that after very slow growth in the early part of the period there was an increase of around 25 per cent between 1780 and 1831, and a subsequent acceleration in the rate of increase.

How new were these phenomena? On the scale of a nation as large as Britain, they were new. On a smaller scale, they were not. The city states of medieval and Renaissance Italy had a

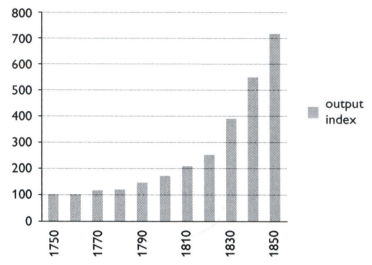

Figure I.1 Growth of industrial output (after Table I.1)

predominance of industry over agriculture, and also represented the growth of urbanism. Urbanism was also triumphant in the monster cities which had grown up in Western Europe since the late medieval period. Of these London, with a population of over half a million people by 1700, was the largest. So neither industrialisation nor urbanisation were new. But it is mechanisation and factories which the ordinary person most associates with the Industrial Revolution and which were least in evidence in past times. Even mechanisation had a precedent, however, for wind- and watermills, both quite complex pieces of machinery, were already ubiquitous in more developed countries, while there had already been developments in textile machinery. On the other hand, well into the nineteenth century Britain was surprisingly unmechanised by today's standards. In 1850 there were 600,000 workers, men and women, in textile factories, about 6 per cent of the total workforce. But 1.8 million men still worked on the land, and most industrial workers still used hand tools rather than minding machines. So while the scale of mechanisation between 1750 and 1850 was greater than anything that had been seen before, the biggest change was actually to come in the next one hundred years. The growth in income per person was not new: there had been such periods of growth in the

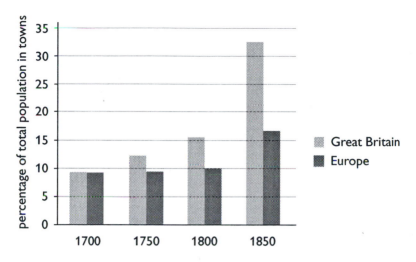

Figure I.2 Urbanisation (after Table I.3)

past. But in the past, periods of growth were usually associated with a decline in population which allowed existing resources to be spread among fewer people. A growth in personal income while population also rose rapidly was a novel phenomenon.

Many of the changes which characterised industrialisation in Britain were not new; but they were unprecedented in scale. Nowhere else, at least in Europe, had ever seen the volume of industry and the size of urban areas which existed in Britain by 1850. Nowhere else had ever seen the concentration of machines which by then existed in the factories of Lancashire. And if to those things is added the extensive use of coal, which cast a pall of smoke over many of the cities and industrial areas, then it is hardly surprising that by the 1840s the phrase 'Industrial Revolution' was coming into common use.

Terminology

Invention and innovation The use of these terms is often somewhat flexible. I have taken invention to mean a novel idea which leads to the devising of a new technique or prototype (in the case of machinery) – thus it covers non-mechanical changes; and innovation to mean the incorporation of such new techniques or machines in the production of goods or the supply of services, or alternatively the supply of a new product – which might itself be the fruit of an invention. (See also Chapter 1 for further discussion and Schumpeter's concept of innovation.)

Money values   It is impossible to translate exactly eighteenth- or nineteenth-century money values into those of today, because the composition of products has changed so much. To simplify, mid-eighteenth-century price levels were about one-hundredth of today's (1999). There was rapid inflation in the 1790s and prices more or less doubled; after 1815 they fell again and by 1850 were back to about 25 per cent above their 1750 level. Average incomes today have gone up by far more than prices, of course. All examples of individual prices and incomes in the text are at their original level. Index numbers in tables may be in current or constant (adjusted for inflation) prices, as indicated.

Profit, superprofit and supernormal profit   The everyday or busi-nessman's definition of profit would be the amount earned by a firm after expenses, and the rate of profit the proportion this bears to the capital employed. The economist would deduct the sum the firm's cap-ital would earn in a risk-free employment, such as loans to the govern-ment; 'profit' therefore becomes the return to risk. In the context of this book it can be taken that, when profit is regarded from the busi-nessman's point of view, the everyday definition is used, and when from the economic point of view the economist's. Both businessmen and economists would agree that risky investments would be expected to earn more profit, and conversely there was at this time a concept of a normal rate of profit, the return expected on an investment of aver-age risks. Superprofits or supernormal profits are profit rates which are higher than normal even though no extra risk is involved. They are likely to be achieved temporarily when demand exceeds supply, caus-ing prices to rise, or when costs suddenly fall; in a free market firms will compete superprofits away but if there are barriers to new entrants or other longer-term disequilibrating factors, then some firms will have a favourable market position and will continue to earn superprofits. (See also Chapter 1 for Schumpeter's concept of profit.)

Working class, middle class and upper class   These terms are used in this book to denote different groups in the population whose socio-economic positions were as they are commonly understood today. The terms contain no implication about such groups' political orientations or the contemporaneous understanding of their economic position.

Tables

Table I.1 Growth of industrial output

	Output growth (index)	Industry's share of the workforce
1750	100	
1760	101	24%
1770	114	
1780	118	
1790	145	
1800	171	29%
1810	205	
1820	249	
1830	387	
1840	545	47%
1850	714	

Sources: Crafts and Harley, 'Output growth', Table A3.1, 'Revised best guess' (see Appendix), and Crafts, British Economic Growth (see Further Reading)

Table I.2 Output in selected industries

	I	II	III
1750	2.3 (1.0)	28 (29)	14.1 (14.4)
1775	6.1 (2.7)	48 (49)	18.0 (18.4)
1800	51.6 (23.2)	180 (184)	19.5 (19.9)
1825	167.0 (75.0)	580 (592)	26.1 (26.6)
1850	588.0 (265.0)	2,225 (2,269)	29.6 (30.2)

After B.R. Mitchell, British Historical Statistics (Cambridge, 1988)

I   raw cotton consumption (i.e. imports less re-exports) in million lb (kg)
II   pig iron production in thousand tons (tonnes)
III glass production in thousand tons (tonnes) (final year is 1845)

Table I.3 Urbanisation

Percentage of total population in towns	1700	1750	1800	1850
Great Britain (over 10,000 inhabitants)	9.4	12.3	15.6	32.5
Europe (over 10,000 inhabitants)	9.2	9.5	10.0	16.7
Great Britain (over 2,500 inhabitants)	18.2	24.2	30.1	50.3

After J. de Vries, *European Urbanisation 1500–1800* (1984), Tables 3.7, 3.8, 4.9

Further reading

There are a number of good histories of the Industrial Revolution period which allocate much more space than the present book to the various sectors and subsectors of the economy, including agriculture and services. Of recent ones M. J. Daunton, *Progress and Poverty: Economic and Social History of Britain 1700–1850* (Oxford, 1995) is comprehensive; P. Hudson, *The Industrial Revolution* (1992) is briefer but still thorough, and contains a useful chapter on the historiography of the Industrial Revolution; J. Rule, *The Vital Century: England's Developing Economy 1714–1815* (1992), and *Albion's People: English Society 1714–1815* (1992) are useful surveys; C. More, *The Industrial Age: Economy and Society in Britain 1750–1995* (2nd ed., 1997) covers the Industrial Revolution period more succinctly than the above. M. Berg, *The Age of Manufactures 1700–1820: Industry, Innovation and Work in Britain 1700–1820* (2nd ed., 1994) is less of a straightforward textbook but is good on work, the division of labour and the textile and metal industries. R. Floud and D. McCloskey, *The Economic History of Britain since 1700*, vol. 1 (2nd ed., Cambridge, 1994) is a strange book: there are individual chapters of great value, but they overlap and are often contradictory, while the book has surprising gaps; for instance, there is practically nothing on transport.

Two more specialised books of great value are C. H. Lee, *The British Economy since 1700: A Macroeconomic Perspective* (Cambridge 1986), which is particularly useful for regional development and the service industries; and N. Crafts, *British Economic Growth during the Industrial Revolution* (Oxford, 1985) which, apart from pioneering a reinterpretation of growth rates discussed in the Appendix, has much on the structure of the economy.

Chapter 1

Models of the Industrial Revolution

Land, labour and capital

The various attempts to explain the Industrial Revolution can be described as 'models'. An historical/economic 'model' is a simplified way of representing a set of economic processes – in this case, those processes which brought about the Industrial Revolution. The model provides a schematic outline which maps the broad sweep of reality – or of what the deviser of the model thinks is reality. Behind the models there are economic theories which explain why the processes outlined in the model should lead to economic growth. Theories differ, however, which is one reason for disagreement between writers on economic growth; another is the schematic nature of models, which means that it is difficult to construct a model which is simple, but is also a sufficient representation of reality. These two potential reasons for disagreement help to explain why it is so difficult to achieve consensus about the Industrial Revolution.

Underlying all the models is the concept of factors of production: land, labour and capital. Land appears self-explanatory as the essential medium for agricultural output. But the economist's land also includes the minerals below the earth's surface, and the latent power of wind and water; paradoxically, it also includes the fruits of the sea. In effect, 'land' to economists is shorthand for all the products of the natural world. Labour is more straightforward, since we all understand what work is; but there are complexities because workers can be more or less skilled. Capital has a dual meaning, as the funds which are used to finance some productive asset, and the asset itself. Capital assets include buildings to house machinery, the machinery itself, mines and other

expensive items; and also such less obvious assets as the crafts-
man's tools, the farmer's seedcorn, and the factory owner's stocks
of raw cotton.

Simple economic growth, without industrialisation, can be
achieved by adding inputs of one or more of these different
factors. Most economists would agree that such simple addition
of factors is also necessary for industrialisation, but they would
add that something else is needed: more efficient use of one or
more of the factors. There are various ways in which this may be
achieved.

It can be achieved through the advantages of size, usually known
as economies of scale or increasing returns. For instance, as ships
increase in size, their cargo capacity grows at a faster rate than their
weight, and so the capital cost of building a bigger ship does not rise
as fast as its cargo capacity. Nor does its crew size, and therefore the
labour of the crew is used more efficiently and crew costs per tonne
carried will be smaller. In economists' jargon, capital productivity
and labour productivity will both be raised. In the same sort of way,
as roads become more intensively used, the capital cost of building
them is spread over more vehicles; and if tolls are charged on the
road, the tollgate keeper opens the gate more often, rather than just
hanging about waiting for the occasional cart. Again, capital and
labour productivity are both increased. If the new road also enables
the land nearby to be cultivated more intensively because the
produce is cheaper to take to market, then land productivity will be
increased too. These examples could be multiplied over almost
every industry and activity.

Economies of scale do not apply only to individual capital
assets such as ships and roads. In a growing economy, there will
be more economic transactions between individuals and firms.
As the number of transactions multiplies, all sorts of savings
enable assets and labour to be used more effectively. For
instance, ships will spend less time waiting in port for a cargo as
traffic grows; more letters will be written and it becomes worth
establishing a postal service, which cuts the cost of exchanging
commercial information. The reduction in transaction costs, of
which transport costs are an important part, is a significant
economy arising from growth. Postal services are examples of
the beneficial civic activities that a larger economy makes
possible. Others are the provision of lighthouses and charts to

aid navigation, and of effective military forces to discourage unfriendly foreign powers or pirates. Sometimes these activities can only be financed by taxation and have to be left to the government, in which case they are known as public goods. Reductions in transaction costs, public goods and other benefits which are external to the firm are collectively known as external economies or beneficial externalities.

Another way in which factors can be used more effectively is summed up in the phrase 'gains from trade'. At its simplest, this expresses the principle that if two partners, each producing a different product more cheaply than the other, exchange those products, both partners will gain so long as transaction costs are lower than the saving in production costs. Such gains can occur through internal and foreign trade. Thus if Lancashire produces cotton cloth and uses resources economically to do so, and East Anglia produces wheat with similar efficiency, they will exchange these goods and each will benefit. The theory of comparative advantage develops the analysis by showing that different partners will maximise income by specialising in products in which they have the greatest relative, or comparative, advantage. Thus even if Britain produced both cotton cloth and wheat using fewer factors of production than France, it would suit Britain to concentrate on producing the one in which its efficiency advantage over France was greatest. If that was cotton cloth, then irrespective of its efficiency advantage in both commodities, Britain would specialise in cloth and exchange it for wheat.

Greater efficiency in factor use can also be achieved by innovation – the adoption of a change which yields a more effective use of resources or provides some new service or item of consumption. Resources might be used more effectively because of a newly-invented machine or through an improvement in organisation. An example of the second is the spread in the eighteenth century of institutions known as turnpike trusts. These levied tolls on roads, enabling more money to be spent on maintenance and new building: thus vehicles could be heavier and go faster, and as a result, the productivity of carriages and waggons (capital), and that of their drivers (labour), increased. Improvement is often achieved through 'learning-by-doing': a simple name which describes exactly what is meant. A machine or a process might have its efficiency improved not by any sort of physical change or new type of organisation, but just by incremental improvement of what is already there. For instance, as engineers in textile mills gained experience they found they could work their steam engines harder and so drive more machinery with the same engine. There was no new technology and no investment was required: it is an example of pure learning-by-doing. (It is possible to distinguish different types of learning-by-doing – for instance, learning-by-making and learning-by-using – but to avoid complexity these will be subsumed under learning-by-doing.)

All the above types of change could be described as process innovations. Product innovation is also important. A new product might appeal to consumers – as did cotton clothing when it was introduced – or it might be a product which is primarily of commercial or industrial importance. New types of insurance, for example, might reduce the risks of foreign trade and thus its cost. It is important to stress the wide nature of innovation. The headlines about the Industrial Revolution have been made by the great inventions – Watt's steam engine, the various textile machines, and so on. The term innovation encompasses the adoption of these, but also the other less spectacular types of change mentioned above.

The factors of production, and the concept that their productivity can be increased, are the main building blocks of the growth models of economists and historians. The models put the blocks together in various ways and sometimes add other components, and it is these various combinations which are described below.

Models of factor accumulation

The simplest growth model points to the increase of capital as the main motor for growth. This encompasses the build-up of assets such as ships, roads, tools and machinery, sometimes known as fixed capital, and also the accumulation of circulating capital. The latter includes, for an individual firm, the stocks of raw material, of goods in the course of production (work-in-progress), and of finished products which have not been sold. It also includes credit the firm has extended to others to enable them to buy its products. For the time being the analysis will focus on the accumulation of fixed capital and will use the term capital assets for this, so that there can be no confusion with capital as an accumulation of funds. But in practice, if capital assets increase, circulating capital is likely to have to increase as well.

To achieve growth in capital assets, their purchase would need to exceed the rate at which they wear out. In economic shorthand, investment would need to exceed depreciation. Land is neglected in this simple growth model because it is ultimately limited in quantity. The world has only so much of it, and so increases in land are not seen as more than temporary reasons for economic growth. An increase in labour supply is neglected because merely increasing the quantity of labour will not necessarily secure a proportionate increase in output. If more people work the same amount of land, with the same amount of fertiliser and the same techniques, output may increase through more intensive cultivation but there will be biological limits to the output increase which can be achieved. If the increased population, instead of working on the land, works in industry, there are similar problems: with no more capital in the form of tools and machinery, output per person grows more slowly than the numbers employed. More and more workers are added, all using the same machines and tools as existing staff; the new recruits get in each other's way and little extra is produced. These likely outcomes are referred to as diminishing returns. As population increases without any increase in land or capital, the additional output generated by each additional worker becomes smaller and smaller, or in other words the marginal productivity of labour is low, or zero. Marginal productivity is an economic concept meaning the additional output added by employing an extra unit – it could be of capital or land, but in this case it is labour; zero marginal productivity of labour means that an extra worker will add no output to the existing total.

With increasing capital, however, output could increase without any growth in either land or labour supplies, and so growth models based on an increase in capital have an intuitive attraction. We associate the Industrial Revolution with capital assets such as textile machines and steam engines, and it seems logical that workers equipped with such assets should produce more. On the other hand, such models do beg fundamental questions. One such is how the additional funds to purchase the assets are acquired. Individuals' savings are one possibility, but savings in pre-industrial societies are usually assumed to be low, so the initial build-up of funds is not easy to explain.

Another problem with simple capital accumulation models is that increments to capital, like additions to labour supply, are liable to diminishing returns if the capital assets employed remain of the same type. For instance, in eighteenth-century Britain only so many stagecoaches could be profitably used; if the number had increased beyond this level, competition would have driven down the return on capital; in other words, the marginal productivity of capital would have fallen. Innovation is particularly important in this context: it counters diminishing returns by raising the return to capital through the opening up of new opportunities for its use. Thus railways opened up many opportunities for profitable capital investment; of course, there were then fewer opportunities for investment in stagecoaches, but railways offered such an advantage to goods and passenger carriage that the capital which could be profitably invested in railways was far greater than that invested in stagecoaches. The point seems obvious but is important because it suggests that growth achieved simply through the increase of capital, without innovation, cannot go on for ever.

In one of the earliest growth models, capital accumulation plays an important part. The other main component of this model is productivity increase occurring because of the development of a market economy: that is an economy in which goods are traded freely, as opposed to a subsistence economy in which producers simply satisfy their own needs. As the market economy develops, it allows the specialisation of function: farmers can grow crops particularly suited to their land and exchange them for other agricultural produce; industries can develop, with their own specialised workforce. Such changes allow people to concentrate on doing one thing, rather than attempt every type of productive activity.

This concentration allows both a reduction in transaction costs and the realisation of gains from trade. In turn, the latter come about partly because of the effective use of human capital. Practice, education and training all develop skills, which can be described as human capital – assets which produce a return from more efficient production. In theory the money spent on these can be measured in the same way as investment in capital assets. If workers concentrate on one activity rather than many, the time spent on training or practice does not necessarily increase; but it is spent more effectively as it is easier to learn one activity than many. The productivity of the investment in human capital is greatly increased. The same principle applies to firms: if they concentrate on one activity, they more quickly develop expertise.

This model is associated in particular with the eighteenth-century Scottish economist Adam Smith – not that Smith would have called it a 'growth model' – and his famous book *The Wealth of Nations*. In Smith's terminology, a more extensive market made possible a greater 'division of labour', which was the key to higher productivity. Innovation is a component of the model – Smith referred to labour-saving machines – but is not essential to it. Nor was a growth in population integral to Smith's model, although it could be incorporated within it. So long as capital increased and land was available, a higher population would increase the volume of exchange and thus make possible a further division of labour. By the early nineteenth century, however, economists such as Thomas Malthus worried that too great an increase in population would pose problems to an economy in which land was fixed in quantity. Diminishing returns would set in and Smith's virtuous circle would become a vicious one.

Smith's model was not a model of the revolutionary change. It was hardly likely to be, because the phrase 'Industrial Revolution' was not coined until after Smith wrote. Smith described a form of growth which had limits: there would have been a point at which no more division of labour could have been profitably achieved because transaction costs would have exceeded the cost-saving benefits of specialisation. If the logic of the model developed by Smith and his pessimistic successors is accepted, how were these limits on growth overcome?

One answer has been suggested recently by Tony Wrigley. Wrigley takes Smith's model as broadly applicable to the growth which took place before the Industrial Revolution. As the eighteenth century wore on, the limits on growth threatened. Wrigley sees them being overcome by the use of inorganic energy in the form of coal. The use of coal freed the old organic economy, reliant on wind-, water-, horse- or humanpower, of a massive constraint. Labour productivity could now grow through the application of steam power to machinery, whether or not the division of labour increased. The limits on agricultural production would be overcome in a number of ways: the use of coal enabled woodland to be turned to food production; transport costs fell due to steam technology, enabling land use to become more specialised than before and also opening up new agricultural land overseas; more efficient production of manufactures enabled Britain to trade manufactures for imported food. In an economic sense, coal was 'land' and thus the use of coal gave Britain a supply of new land. With hindsight we can see that coal and other inorganic energy supplies are ultimately limited, but in the context of the energy needs of the day the supply of coal was virtually unlimited.

Wrigley does not suggest that the two processes – the expansion of the market and the use of coal – were entirely distinct. The two overlapped chronologically, in that coal use in Britain was expanding from the sixteenth century onwards, while the market did not stop expanding in the eighteenth century but has gone on doing so until the present day. But he does suggest that the processes were logically separate. And while he suggests that the growth of the economy after 1750 was increasingly dependent on coal, in his model other changes were necessary to enable growth to continue. Capital assets in coal-related uses, such as the mines themselves and transport systems, had to increase. And invention was essential, for instance in the design of new types of furnace for metal manufacture and in the development of the steam engine.

Another model in which invention and innovation were important was that of Karl Marx, whose most famous book, *Capital*, was published in 1867. Marx is best known for what he said about the effects of the Industrial Revolution, and that will be discussed later. His model of industrialisation sees it as a combination of market expansion, capital accumulation and innovation. Marx's emphasis on the last was exceptional when he wrote in the mid-nineteenth century but, in the light of modern thinking, his ideas about the causes of industrialisation are only distinctive in a few specific ways, notably the mechanism of capital accumulation. He believed that capital accumulation, once industrialisation was under way, occurred because workers were not paid the full value of their labour, thus leaving surplus value which provided funds for investment. Before industrialisation started and provided this mechanism for further capital accumulation, the initial funds needed were provided by the same processes at work in agriculture, and by the exploitation of lands overseas.

Marx's emphasis on capital accumulation is echoed by two theorists with very different political views from his. One was Arthur Lewis, whose model is often known as 'economic development with unlimited supplies of labour', after his article with that title, written in 1954. In this model, there is a subsistence sector in the economy, in which there is surplus labour. In other words, the population has outgrown the capacity of the land to provide productive work. Individual workers are underemployed, that is lacking regular work, and thus the marginal productivity of labour is low or zero. Only additional capital assets could enable productivity to improve, but Lewis posits an absence of capital accumulation in the subsistence sector, so that sector offers no escape from the trap of low labour productivity. Lewis sees the answer in a capitalist sector in which labour productivity is higher because of the employment of capital, in the form of machinery and so on. As this draws its labour from the subsistence sector, it only has to pay a wage which enables workers to maintain the low living standards to which they are accustomed. With high labour productivity and low wages, profits are high. The capitalist sector reinvests these profits in further capital equipment and thus raises labour productivity further. The wage it pays remains the same and thus profits per unit of output increase. As total profits rise, reinvestment becomes more rapid and a virtuous circle of capital accumulation ensues. At some stage surplus labour is used up, wages begin to rise, and while profits will not then increase so fast, the payoff in terms of ordinary people's living standards begins.

In emphasising capital accumulation, Lewis's model has similarities to Marx's although the economic theory underpinning it is quite different. Drawing on both Marx and Lewis is the proto-industrialisation model, developed in the 1970s. According to this view, industry between the sixteenth and eighteenth centuries, particularly the textile industry, moved from the towns, where wages were relatively high, to rural areas. There it made use of low-wage surplus labour, the techniques of production remaining simple and hand-powered: this was 'proto-industry'. The surplus profits could then be reinvested, not necessarily in the textile industry but elsewhere in the economy. While the use of low-wage surplus labour and the reinvestment of surplus profits are obvious similarities to the Lewis model, there are big differences. Lewis saw the capitalist sector as modern and using modern techniques, while in proto-industrialisation theory, capitalists are chiefly marked by their ability to exploit low-wage labour while techniques remain simple.

Another theorist who echoes Marx in his emphasis on capital accumulation is W.W. Rostow in his *The Stages of Economic Growth*, published in 1960. Rostow was explicitly concerned with explaining the Industrial Revolution, although he believed that his growth model also explained the process of industrialisation in other countries. Rostow's 'stages' have been criticised for all sorts of reasons. The main one is that for the most part they are not explanatory but taxonomic, that is they simply list a number of phenomena which Rostow believes have occurred or will occur at various stages of growth. However, this criticism cannot be made about Rostow's crucial stage which is the 'take-off' to a state where economic growth is the 'normal condition'. In Britain, the Industrial Revolution was the take-off stage. Rostow does supply an explanatory model for the take-off, the salient features of which are that a 'leading sector' of industry emerges with a very high growth rate, and investment increases substantially as a proportion of national income.

By 'leading sector' Rostow means an industry which was relatively so important that its rapid growth, and consequent demand for other industrial products, stimulated industrialisation throughout the rest of the economy. In Britain, according to him, cotton textiles was such a leading sector from the 1780s onwards. Not only did it stimulate industrialisation through demand, it also generated high profits which could be used for investment. Rostow suggests various reasons why a leading sector developed in different countries during industrialisation. In Britain, the immediate reason was the rapid reduction in costs and prices, and hence expansion in sales, which resulted from innovation in the cotton textile industry. So while the concept of a leading sector and capital accumulation are the main ingredients of Rostow's model, he believed that in the British Industrial Revolution innovation was also important.

Rostow has been criticised for giving precise percentages for the rise in investment – that it should rise to 10 per cent of national income or more – but these criticisms are unfair. The point he is making is that if investment remains at a low level typical of pre-industrial societies – he suggests 5 per cent – then it will not exceed depreciation and the total assets, known as the capital stock, of the country will not increase. Investment must increase substantially so that the capital stock of the country grows strongly. This will be particularly necessary if the population is growing rapidly. The important thing about this aspect of Rostow's model is not the precise figures but the fact that, like many other theorists, he sees capital accumulation, which results from the high profits available in some parts of the economy, as essential to industrialisation.

Models of entrepreneurship and innovation

There are similarities between Rostow's model and an earlier model of growth put forward by the economist Joseph Schumpeter. However, Schumpeter's ideas also contain important differences of emphasis to all other growth models.

Schumpeter believed that there were two key factors in rapid growth – which he called economic development, to distinguish it from slow and gradual growth which he thought went on most of the time and did not need special explanation. One of these factors was entrepreneurship, the other innovation. In addition, access to credit was a necessary prerequisite. By entrepreneurship, Schumpeter meant something very specific. His habit of inventing his own definitions for familiar words is irritating, but understandable because the word 'entrepreneur' has often been used very loosely and vaguely. Most commentators have tended to view the entrepreneur and the capitalist as more or less the same: they are the people who take a risk by investing their cash in setting up a new business. Schumpeter regarded the provision of such funds and the consequent taking of risk as the role of the capitalist; it was quite separate from the role of the entrepreneur. Entrepreneurship entailed the possession of a special quality of foresight and a heightened ability to seize opportunities. Entrepreneurship was a function: an individual could fulfil it only by possessing these particular attributes. In practice the same person might fulfil the function of entrepreneur and some other function, such as that of capitalist, but equally someone might be an entrepreneur and nothing else.

Clearly the opportunities that the entrepreneur seizes must be specific to economic development. They are opportunities to make a profit, and they arise because of innovation. Here again, Schumpeter had his own definitions. Profit, to him, was not the ordinary return on capital which any capitalist would expect; it was, rather, a higher than normal return, and so Schumpeter's 'profit' was what other economists refer to as supernormal profits. And innovation did not just comprise the opportunity for technical change or reorganisation, but also the opening of new markets and even the development of a new source of supply of raw materials. Innovation was shorthand for any sort of discontinuity. It was these discontinuities which gave rise to profit opportunities. With a new cost-reducing machine, or a new source of supply, the entrepreneur could reduce costs and make a profit, at least until others adopted the same measures. With the opening of new markets, the entrepreneur could widen the demand for his or her goods and make a profit that way. It was not necessary for funds to be built up before the process of innovation, so long as entrepreneurs could persuade capitalists to obtain the necessary credit, which could be created in various ways.

Schumpeter saw economic development in the modern period as a worldwide phenomenon related to huge cycles of economic activity. Therefore he disliked the phrase 'Industrial Revolution' as he saw the period as simply one part, if an important and notable one, of such a cycle. Once a business cycle got under way, and a few industries were growing rapidly, they stimulated demand, and therefore profit opportunities, in others, and so industrialisation spread rapidly as entrepreneurs responded. Unlike Rostow, Schumpeter did not afford primacy to the cotton industry in this process during British industrialisation, although he thought it very important.

The most distinctive feature of Schumpeter's model is his emphasis on entrepreneurship. Of course, other models assume that entrepreneurs do respond to profit opportunities, although Lewis and others use the term capitalist to mean both the supplier of funds and the fulfiller of entrepreneurial functions. But no one else puts the entrepreneur at the forefront as Schumpeter did, or specifies so precisely the nature of the profit opportunities to which the entrepreneur responds. To Schumpeter, these opportunities arise because of innovation in a wide sense, and thus innovation is a key part of his model as it is in other models. Capital accumulation, however, which is important in some other models, was not to Schumpeter a prerequisite for growth but could occur through credit creation. And neither labour supply nor land use were of much significance to him except insofar as new supplies of raw materials, or the opening up of new markets overseas, might afford profit opportunity.

Invention and innovation are ingredients of the majority of the models described above. However, relatively few of these models examine in detail the conditions in which change might come about. Most accounts of the Industrial Revolution attach some importance to the scientific advances that had been made in Europe since the sixteenth century, and perhaps even more to the habits of methodical investigation associated with science. Some historians also stress the development of craft skills in Britain, and a favourable legal and social climate. A model which puts invention at the forefront has been advanced recently by Joel Mokyr. He accepts a broadly Schumpeterian account of change, in which inventions create profit opportunities. Schumpeter, however, regarded inventions *per se* as less important than the entrepreneurs who exploited them. To Mokyr it is the inventions themselves which were crucial. Mokyr divides inventions into macro – the radical new ideas such as the steam engine and the spinning jenny – and micro – the mass of small improvements subsequently made to the macroinventions. In many cases the latter were only made economic by these improvements. He sees the macroinventions of the eighteenth century as dependent to some extent on such factors as were mentioned earlier in the paragraph. Once a number of inventions had been made, there were links between the various technologies which encouraged further change; for instance, steam engines encouraged developments in metalworking technology, which in turn were fostered by better and cheaper iron. However, successful invention was also to some extent random. Before inventions were made, it was not predetermined that they would succeed. The inventor might have had a good idea but gone the wrong way about making it operational – or just an idea which looked good on paper but which would never have been economic. So the large number of successful inventions in the eighteenth century was, in part, a lucky accident.

Mokyr's, and other similar, accounts of the process of invention can be described as exogenous growth theories. They accept that capital accumulation without technical change leads to diminishing returns to capital and thus less incentive to invest. In their view, this state of affairs characterised the period before the Industrial Revolution. The macroinventions of the eighteenth century raised the return on capital and stimulated a rise in investment. The macroinventions were 'exogenous' because they did not occur within the existing framework of economic relationships, but resulted from external factors such as scientific advance, amateur tinkering and sheer accident. On this account, the Industrial Revolution really was revolutionary.

Mokyr himself stresses the receptive environment for invention in Britain, but another model puts even more emphasis on the random nature of invention. It has been put forward by Nick Crafts, whose focus is on the development of the key machines used in the textile industry from the 1770s. Crafts argues that, in the European context, there was no clearly identifiable reason why Britain should have been first in developing these machines. France possessed much scientific expertise, and in the mid-eighteenth century had a substantial textile industry. He suggested that, in these circumstances, the development of effective textile machinery in Britain, rather than France, was a matter of chance. Both countries had the conditions in which inventions could have been successfully made and utilised, but they happened to be made first in Britain. This fortuitous initial advantage gave a few years' start in which a mechanised British cotton industry could establish itself. The French industry was then battered by the Revolution, the loss of France's colonial markets, and war. By 1815, the end of the Napoleonic Wars, the British industry was much larger. This meant that Britain could reap the advantages of specialisation. Its cotton industry now had such low costs, relative to others, that it dominated world markets and thus continued to grow very rapidly.

Crafts does not see the rapid development of the factory-based cotton industry as the only important change in the period, and his views are not therefore aligned with Rostow's. He believes that structural change in the economy, away from agriculture and towards industry, was likely to have occurred anyway. But if the cotton industry had not grown in the way that it did, the popular conception of the Industrial Revolution as involving mechanisation and factories would not have been realised to the same extent.

Growth was likely to have been slower overall and to have taken a different form.

There is an alternative set of views, also developed in recent years, known as endogenous growth theories. Like exogenous growth theories, they wish to explain why returns to capital do not diminish but, instead, remain so attractive that investment as a proportion of national income steadily increases. Endogenous growth theories put the emphasis on inventions occurring within the existing economic context. Invention and innovation can be explained partly by the workings of demand and supply, which motivate inventors, and partly by the existence of human capital and of learning-by-doing. On this account, Britain was well placed during the Industrial Revolution in that it had a relatively large number of engineers and mechanics who could both make big inventions, and also develop these into practical use via numerous microinventions, which often came about through learning-by-doing. Endogenous growth theorists, therefore, stress the importance of human capital formation: this encouraged the continued development and application of macro- and microinventions, thus ensuring that physical capital investment in the Industrial Revolution did not suffer from diminishing returns.

Although proponents of the different theories are, at the time of writing, engaged in hot debate in the pages of economic history journals, both sides recognise that the two views can accommodate each other to some extent. For instance, most exogenous growth theorists would accept that there is a considerable role for human capital formation. And both theories differ from the majority of models so far reviewed in that they take the availability of capital more or less for granted, and therefore put no emphasis on its initial accumulation. In this they have much in common with Schumpeter. However, unlike Schumpeter, who believed in the fundamental importance of the entrepreneurs who adopted inventions, modern theories consider the inventions themselves central, whilst disagreeing over their causes.

The thrust of all the models of growth considered so far, and the theories on which they are based, has been an emphasis on change in the supply side of the economy. Increases in capital assets, or innovation, or other changes have lowered the cost of production, thus creating profit opportunities and incentives for further investment. Broadly speaking, the demand for goods subject to such supply-side changes is assumed to have already existed or been latent. As the costs and prices of these goods fell, people consumed more of them; spending would have switched from some other commodity, but as the economy moved on to a higher plane of activity and efficiency, incomes rose and total demand increased. Supply created its own demand, an epigram known as 'Say's Law' after the French economist who was said to have formulated it.

Demand-side models

There is another way of looking at growth, which is to start with demand. Additional demand sends out market signals: prices rise, or businessmen anticipate their rise, and are motivated to invest. Various causes of such demand increase have been suggested: in particular population growth, foreign trade and war.

The period 1750–1850 saw an unprecedented growth in Britain's population, from seven and a half million to over twenty million, and this has often been seen as a motor for economic growth. However, the earlier discussion suggests that rising population by itself will run into diminishing returns. There will be more people but they will be poorer. One possible counter-argument is that population growth actually encouraged capital formation. Growth in the demand for housing, for example, pushed up rents and there-fore encouraged house-building; across the entire economy, the return to capital was raised, with a consequent inducement to invest. The demand stimulus did not have the same effect on wages, because the rising population kept wages low – a Lewis-like effect on the supply price of labour.

This is essentially a Keynesian-type analysis, known as such because of the influence of the economist J.M. Keynes. In his famous book of 1936, *The General Theory of Employment, Interest and Money*, Keynes postulated a state of affairs in which opportunities for investment did not match the propensity, that is the desire, to save. In these circumstances, incomes would fall to produce a level of saving which equalled investment (since the two must be equal except insofar as savings are absorbed by hoarding or loans to the government). Therefore national income (and output, which equates to income) would fall and the new level of output would be below the level at which all who wished to work would be fully employed. In Keynes's model, as in Lewis's, labour might be unemployed; but to Keynes the underlying problem was not shortage of capital but an inability to find profitable use for it.

Keynes was mainly concerned to explain the unemployment of the 1920s and 1930s but his analysis could be extended backwards in time. Since in Keynesianism investment comes first and savings second, the low level of capital accumulation in the early eighteenth century could be explained as a result of diminishing returns to capital which limited profit opportunities, in turn discouraging investment, rather than as a result of insufficient savings. Once the demand from the rising population had used up the capacity of existing capital assets, there would be an incentive to invest more: the savings to finance this would be forthcoming from the higher incomes earned by producers.

Keynesian analysis assumes a closed economy, that is it does not consider exports; but on the assumption of surplus capital and labour, exports could be another source of demand stimulus. If capital and labour were already fully employed, then the increase in export demand would simply draw them away from other production. But if there was underemployment, export demand would draw factors into employment without output falling elsewhere. Capital would then increase because, as in the case of population growth, the increased profit opportunities would encourage businessmen to invest more.

There is one obvious problem with overseas trade as a stimulus to industrialisation: it was frequently interfered with by war. From 1750 to 1815 Britain was officially at war: 1756–63 (the Seven Years' War), 1776–83 (the American War of Independence) and 1793–1815 (the Revolutionary and Napoleonic Wars, often called the French Wars), the last with brief breaks which hardly dented their overall impact. All these wars involved disruption to trade, although they also offered opportunities for Britain to seize new markets.

War had a number of other possible economic consequences. If the government's expenditure on war products, and on soldiers' and sailors' wages, came from taxation, it reduced incomes and thus consumer spending and possibly saving; if from loans, it absorbed savings; if from short-term credit, it might be inflationary, raising prices but not raising incomes to the same extent, and thus eventually reducing consumer spending and saving by a more roundabout route. These effects might simply mean that any boost to government spending from war was cancelled out by reductions in spending elsewhere. The effects on savings might be more serious, and analysis usually concentrates on these. In this scenario investment, being directly dependent on savings, fell as savings fell, with deleterious effects on growth. Investment was 'crowded out', and crowding-out is the name given to this effect. Historians who have pointed to its possible existence tend to think that wars were bad for growth.

Keynesian assumptions, however, suggest that government spending on war might have had positive economic effects. In the same way as would population growth or exports, war spending stimulated demand and therefore investment. Again, the supposition is that labour was underemployed and that the tendency to save exceeded the tendency to invest. As investment rose, savings rose because of enhanced incomes, thus providing further funds for investment and for government spending too. Crowding-out would be much less likely to happen, since investment was not dependent on prior savings. Of course, war was only good for growth if there was a lack of investment opportunities elsewhere.

Another possible method of demand stimulus would have involved a shift in tastes by some or all of the population. 'Taste', to economists, has a specific meaning which is wider than its normal usage: 'preference' is the nearest everyday equivalent. Historians have often suggested a connection between a shift in tastes and industrialisation. Maybe there was a shift of tastes from leisure (or idleness, depending on your point of view) to consumption of goods and services, thus stimulating demand. Alternatively, tastes may have shifted from traditional goods to goods in modern industries – for instance, from pewter, the traditional material for tableware, towards earthenware. It has sometimes been suggested that pre-industrial consumers were so conservative that they were reluctant to shift their patterns of spending. If this is accepted, it was necessary for consumers' basic attitudes to change before industrialisation got under way.

A similar effect could have been achieved by a change in the distribution of income. If, for example, the middle classes had consumed the bulk of industrial consumer goods in the first place, and their incomes had increased at the expense of poorer groups, then the demand for such goods would have risen at the expense of whatever goods were most consumed by the poor – probably food.

There are no quick answers to the problem of understanding the Industrial Revolution. Competing economic theories and the simplifications inherent in model-building ensure plentiful disagreement. The historian's job is not to adjudicate between economic theories, although he can be guided by others; but the historian can indicate where reality, or as near as we can get to it when studying the past, conflicts or agrees with the models. That is the task of the following chapters.

Further reading

For economic theorists, particularly Marx and Keynes, a very useful source is Mark Blaug, *Economic Theory in Retrospect*, (4th ed., Cambridge, 1984). For Lewis there is no substitute for the original article: W.A. Lewis, 'Economic development with unlimited supplies of labour', *The Manchester School*, 22 (1954), pp. 139–91; it is reprinted in full in M. Gersovitz, *Selected Economic Writings of W.A. Lewis* (New York, 1983), pp. 311–64. It is often assumed that Lewis was only writing about modern-day developing countries. In fact, Lewis believed that his ideas were generally applicable to industrialisation, including the Industrial Revolution; see pp. 156 and 158 of the original article, and p. 155 for the acerbic comment that 'We cannot explain any "industrial" revolution (as the economic historians pretend to do) until we can explain why saving increased relatively to national income'. As with Lewis, Schumpeter is endlessly referred to but rarely discussed in detail. His most accessible work is J.A. Schumpeter, *The Theory of Economic Development* (Cambridge, Mass., 1934), originally published in 1912; *Business Cycles*, vol. 1 (New York, 1939) adds masses of detail but not much else. Schumpeter is not easy to read and can be dull, but is often fascinating. Adam Smith is almost always interesting: A. Smith, *The Wealth of Nations* is available in various editions. A guide such as Blaug is recommended for Marx: vol. I of *Capital* was published in 1867; vol.s II and III much later, after Marx's death. There are numerous later editions. Moving to more recent theorists, N.F.R. Crafts' article, 'Industrial revolution in England and France: some thoughts on the question, "Why was England first?"', *EcHR*, 30 (1977), pp. 429–41, is still worth reading; the author has written much since, referred to elsewhere, and his original strongly exogenous ideas have tended to be overshadowed. However, they still lurk in his more recent writings. See Crafts, 'Exogenous or endogenous growth? the industrial revolution reconsidered', *JEH*, 55 (1995), pp. 745–72 and a subsequent debate: D. Greasley and L. Oxley, 'Endogenous growth or "Big Bang": two views of the first industrial revolution', *JEH*, 57 (1997), pp. 935–49; Crafts and T.C. Mills, 'Endogenous innovation, trend growth and the

British industrial revolution', *Ibid.*, pp. 950–56 and a final rejoinder by Greasley and Oxley, 'Endogenous growth, trend output and the industrial revolution', *Ibid.*, pp. 957–60. For endogenous growth see also A. Young, 'Invention and bounded learning by doing', *Journal of Political Economy*, 100 (1993), pp. 443–72. For long-term theories of change J.L. Anderson, *Explaining Long-term Economic Change* (1991) is useful while J.D. Gould, *Economic Growth in History* (1972) is very good on more theoretical aspects of growth.

L.A. Clarkson, *Proto-industrialisation: The First Phase of Industrialisation?* (1985).

J. Mokyr, *Levers of Riches: Technological Creativity and Economic Progress* (Oxford, 1990).

W.W. Rostow, *The Stages of Economic Growth: A Non-Communist Manifesto* (Cambridge, 1960).

E.A. Wrigley, *Continuity, Chance and Change: The Character of the Industrial Revolution in England* (Cambridge, 1988).

Chapter 2

Capital accumulation

In a number of the models of industrialisation outlined above, capital accumulation plays a vital part. It is particularly important in the models of Marx, Lewis and Rostow, and it is also integral to Schumpeter's. The available figures suggest that the rate of accumulation, and the total volume of investment, grew impressively throughout the Industrial Revolution period.

The rapid advance of mechanisation is integral to the popular image of the Industrial Revolution, but in fact, machinery was a very small part of total investment. A substantial amount took the form of increases of stocks of raw material and goods in various stages of production, that is circulating capital, although as industrialisation proceeded this became less important. Around one-third of investment in the late eighteenth century was in agriculture, one-fifth in housing, and only a quarter in industry and trade, of which much was stockbuilding. Transport was also important. By 1830 the agricultural share had halved and one-third of a much larger total went into trade and industry. Even this proportion seems low but it is important to remember that economic growth needs all types of investment. Transport is essential to industry while workers need houses, particularly if they move to new areas of work such as towns.

Investment is financed by savings, although whether savings are causally prior to investment is a matter of debate. Individuals could save and lend their money to others, who invested it in capital assets. This could be done without an intermediary, for instance through a mortgage, that is a loan secured on assets; or it could be done by placing the savings in a bank or with some other intermediary which then lent them on to others. Alternatively, savings could be applied direct to investment. This would occur if a firm was started by individuals using their own savings, or if the surplus cash of an existing enterprise was used to buy further assets. The latter, often known as ploughback, is at the root of Lewis's model of capital accumulation. Lewis thought that capitalist firms would be most likely to do this, but in theory peasant farms or one-person enterprises could plough back their surplus cash. Governments could invest directly. And a final method of raising money for investment is through credit creation, by banks or by other means.

Investment

Of these methods of financing investment, the government was the least important during the Industrial Revolution. Central government invested very little in economically productive assets: a few roads and canals, such as the Royal Military Canal from Rye in Sussex to Shorncliffe in Kent, were constructed for strategic reasons; but they were quite unimportant for commercial purposes. Central government constructed buildings for its own purposes, such as the new Palace of Westminster in the 1830s and 1840s, or for defence. But whatever indirect economic effect these had, by promoting stable government in Britain and the defence of the realm, is not measurable. The main investment the government made which was likely to have had an economic impact, although again an indirect one, was capital spending on schools: by developing literacy, this would have enhanced human capital. Government support started in 1833, when it began to make building grants to the existing voluntary providers. However, this comes too late in our period for its impact to have been significant.

Local government did make more investments of economic significance. Road construction was largely done by turnpike trusts, but a considerable amount of road maintenance was still the responsibility of local authorities. However, maintenance, necessary though it was, did not constitute new investment. At best it counteracted the depreciation of existing assets and therefore increased the room for some of the funds raised by the turnpikes to be spent on new construction. More significant than road maintenance was investment in paving, lighting, sewerage and water

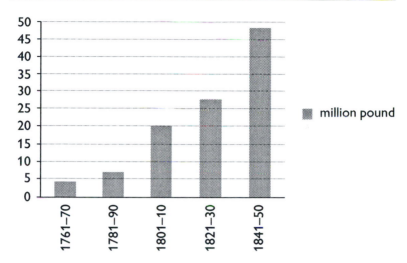

Figure 2.1 Investment (after Table 2.1)

supplies in urban areas. While investments in these were substantial, they were only a small part of total capital investment.

Turnpike trusts, canal companies and later railway companies provided the transport infrastructure. A small beginning had been made on improving this with river navigations, whose purpose is self-explanatory, in the seventeenth century. Turnpikes then developed, with expansion at its most rapid between 1750 and 1770. The first canals were built in the mid-eighteenth century but their peak period of construction was 1780–1815. Primitive railways had been in existence for a long time but, as large-scale capital projects, they only took off in the 1820s, with construction accelerating rapidly in the 1830s to a peak in the 1840s. So throughout the whole of the Industrial Revolution period one type of transport mode or another was being actively developed, although there were peaks and troughs of activity within the periods given above.

The initial finance for these projects was raised through some variation on the pattern of individuals saving and lending their money to others to invest. Turnpikes were trusts, a method of incorporating non-profit enterprises. They took over existing roads and improved them, or built new ones, collecting revenue by way of tolls. Being non-profit-making, they were financed by loan capital paying a fixed rate of interest. Most turnpikes maintained their roads adequately and successful ones with more revenue could plough back surplus cash into more improvements. Canals were financed by a mixture of loan capital paying a fixed rate of interest, and shares on which dividends were paid which reflected profits, the latter predominating. Railways were financed in the same way but usually with a higher proportion of loan capital.

Fixed-interest loans were a familiar type of investment because the government had issued large amounts of such loans since the late seventeenth century. These were known as annuities or stocks. Nowadays they would be called bonds. There was an element of risk in that stocks could fluctuate in value, broadly speaking in inverse correlation to the current rate of interest. And, of course, any commercial undertaking might fail to earn enough revenue to pay interest at the stated rate. Nevertheless turnpike trust loans and other fixed-interest loans were usually safe 'widows and orphans' type securities. Shares were also familiar because the Bank of England and the East India Company were financed in this way and their shares were widely held. These two companies' shares were reckoned very safe investments, and as a result, they and government stocks were known collectively as the Funds. Most shares were more speculative, railway and some canal shareholders enjoying, or suffering, the effect of gearing. The interest on the loan capital had to be paid first: so if earnings were good, dividends on shares were likely to be high; but if they were bad, dividends could shrink or disappear. (Shares were also known at this time as stock, a usage carried down in the American term 'common stock'; in Britain the term 'equities' is more familiar.)

Today equities provide a large proportion of the finance of most companies of any size. From the early eighteenth to the mid-nineteenth centuries, however, their issue was largely confined to canals and railways. The Bubble Act of 1720, following the notorious financial scandal of the South Sea Bubble, had made it necessary for companies issuing shares, called joint-stock companies, to do so through a private Act of Parliament, the idea being to discourage speculation. Thus canals and railways had to have such Acts. This may have discouraged other firms from incorporating, that is becoming joint-stock companies. But since the repeal of the Bubble Act in 1825 did not lead to large numbers of new incorporations, except among banks, it seems that most firms did not conceive of themselves as likely to grow so much as to need a joint-stock structure.

The majority of firms were financed in other ways. Most started with money subscribed by an individual, or several partners, who already had some wealth. Thus ships, at the beginning of the period, were usually owned by partners who invested different sums of money. The capital for banks usually came from well-off provincial manufacturers and merchants. And in diverse industries wealthy individuals would diversify their existing interests by starting new firms: George Philips, for example, inherited a successful hat-making firm and also had textile interests, then became a partner in a Manchester cotton-spinning business in 1791. Subsequently he started other businesses. Philips was already very wealthy and most of those who started banks were well off, but investors in ships often had quite modest means, as did those who started up in many other lines of activity, for instance the West Riding woollen industry. What was difficult, however, was to start up anything but the smallest firm without some existing capital. Once a firm had been started, there was a common pattern in which early profits were largely reinvested in the firm, assuming that it had some degree of success. (Shipowning was different, because each ship was in effect a separate firm and needed little reinvestment; as time went by, however, specialised large-scale shipping firms developed.)

In rapidly expanding industries this pattern of early plough-back would hold even if the firm itself was not expanding. Most industries which expanded rapidly were those, such as textiles, in which technology was also changing fast. In these circumstances cash had to be ploughed back merely to survive. As industries matured and the rate of change slowed, there was less need to invest merely to survive, so long as the firm in question was reasonably successful. Such firms generated surplus cash for their owners, who often wished to diversify their assets. The motive for this is often said to be the reduction of risk and the need to provide a secure income for relatives without other means of support. Sometimes, however, the motive seems to have been the lure of starting off again in a new, perhaps risky, but potentially lucrative business. So while a few firms chose to single-mindedly expand within one industry, the majority of owners preferred to invest surplus cash elsewhere. One of the most famous start-ups was promoted by a well-established woollen manufacturer-cum-banker, Edward Pease of Darlington, in the northeast. This was the Stockton and Darlington railway of 1825, the line which popularised steam haulage. In moving to a new and untried sector of business Pease was taking far more of a risk than if he had stayed with his existing businesses. Diversification did not necessarily equal risk aversion.

While most successful businessmen started with some wealth and ploughed back a proportion of their surplus cash, many also needed to borrow. Predictably, smaller businessmen seem to have had most need to do this. One of the standard means of raising cash was the mortgage, a legal device giving the lender security over land or buildings. Loans on mortgages were usually advanced for a limited period, such as a year. From the lender's point of view, they were less liquid than bonds, that is they were less easily turned into cash; but conversely, their capital value did not fluctuate with interest rates, since the capital could be reclaimed at full value when the term of the mortgage expired. The great advantage of the mortgage for both lender and borrower was its security. This was a reassurance to the lender, and enabled the loan to be made at a relatively low rate of interest which was an advantage to the borrower. Mortgages, therefore, were also loans in which 'widows and orphans' and all those seeking security could put their savings. Their cheapness was aided by their simplicity and familiarity. Attorneys, the eighteenth-century equivalent of solicitors, usually arranged mortgages, having good contacts with potential lenders and borrowers; in the West Riding of Yorkshire they were arranged for a fee of one-quarter per cent of the principal.

Mortgages were often used to finance purchases or improvement of agricultural land, but they were also important in industry. An individual with some land – and many small producers in the Yorkshire woollen industry, for example, were also small landowners – could borrow money on the security of their land to enlarge their business or start a new one. Alternatively, a businessman could purchase land or buildings for his business with cash and then mortgage them, thus raising more money to finance machinery or circulating capital. Another important activity which was financed by mortgage was house-building. Large numbers of people, down to the level of artisans, developed housing, at least on a small scale. Relatively small amounts of money were needed to start with, further sums being raised by mortgage as houses were built.

Banks are nowadays the main lenders to industrial and commercial customers, but in 1750 banks barely existed outside London and Scotland. By the late eighteenth century 'country' banks, that is banks in England outside London, were growing rapidly in number and becoming increasingly important as providers of industrial capital. Technically banks only lent short-term, but in practice they would allow overdrafts to run on from year to year, thus effectively lending long-term. More important, businessmen often had other sources of long-term finance, as noted above, and bank loans were most useful to finance fluctuations in stocks and debtors – circulating capital. Bank funds originated in various ways. First, banks acted as straightforward intermediaries between savers and investors: money was deposited and then lent out. Insofar as they did this, banks were doing little more than attorneys who arranged loans. The advantage of banks was that they were more flexible, having a pool of money which allowed the addition or subtraction of small amounts as savings or borrowings. They made saving and borrowing a bit easier, and perhaps a bit cheaper, for some people, but did not change the essentials of the process, and many people continued to lend and borrow on mortgages in the old way. By the turn of the century a new pool of money was becoming available for lending to capital-hungry growth areas. These were savings from slow-growing areas with less demand for investment. Specialist intermediaries in London organised the transfer of such surplus funds, which were important in financing certain activities, for example the export trade in Yorkshire woollens.

Finally, banks were also creators of credit. The very act of bank lending was likely to lead to this. A bank would receive a deposit in gold or in Bank of England notes; the deposit would be lent to a borrower, but the loan might not be in gold or Bank of England notes. (In 1797 wartime inflation and the strain on the balance of payments forced Britain to end the requirement that cash transactions should be made in gold, if that was demanded. Bank of England notes became the basic currency, along with small coin, until Britain returned to gold in 1821.) A bank loan might take the form of a country bank's own notes, which up to the 1820s such banks could freely issue. Or it could take the form of a bill, accepted by the bank, to discharge some other debt of the borrower. Bills were orders, accepted by a 'drawee' who was then liable to pay the money by a certain date. Since the bank still had the depositor's gold to meet immediate claims for cash, it might choose to advance more money than the original deposit. Such advances, if in notes and bills, constituted claims on the depositor which might eventually have to be met in gold. Balancing the need to keep some gold with the profitability which came from increasing advances was the banker's skill.

Banks thus played an increasing role both in matching savers to borrowers and in credit creation. As time went by London and country banks were supplemented by larger joint-stock banks, authorised from 1826. But before the late eighteenth century banks were of little importance in financing industry, and they were never important in financing house-building or transport. For much of the period, furthermore, credit creation also went on outside the banking sector. It occurred through the acceptance of bills by merchants and manufacturers, and so long as the individual concerned was of good name, the bill would pass virtually as cash. In effect, someone in such a position could create their own credit: they could issue a bill with which they could command resources without immediately paying cash. The receiver of the bill could in turn 'accept' it, thus also becoming liable, and so a bill would circulate, becoming a better risk as it collected more signatures. Such bills were limited to the extent that some personal knowledge of one of the acceptors was needed by the holder of the bill; but in small geographical areas where there was active trade this was not a problem. In both Lancashire and Yorkshire, bills were common currency in the late eighteenth century, providing numerous businessmen with the equivalent of cash. Bills circulated throughout the local economy, since firms of all sizes extended credit, often for three months or more, to their customers.

How can we link the preceding outline of the volume of investment and the means by which savings were transmitted to investors with the models described in Chapter 1? Marx and Lewis saw the increase in capital accumulation as a bedrock of the Industrial Revolution. It was the work of capitalists who both made the savings because of the high profits they earned and then used these savings for investment. Exogenous and endogenous growth

theories focus on the attractiveness of investment. The prior existence of savings is not seen as a major problem. There might,
however, be another way in which savings accumulated and were
linked with investment.

There had always been some saving to finance the moderate level
of investment which took place. In the early eighteenth century the
groups which saved were the landowners, large farmers,
merchants, manufacturers, and the rest of the middle classes – small
shopkeepers and tradesmen, yeomen farmers, professionals and
those who had inherited wealth. Such groups already had an
income sufficient for their basic consumption needs and so it seems
likely that if their incomes grew they would increase the proportion
which they set aside to provide for retirement or a rainy day. In
economic terms they had a high marginal propensity to save, and so
savings would have risen more steeply than incomes. The model
assumes neither unlimited supplies of labour nor the availability of
above-normal profits through innovation. It merely assumes that
interest rates were stable, so that saving became neither more nor
less attractive at constant rates of income. As there was some
growth in income per person in the early eighteenth century,
savings, on this assumption, rose faster (see Figure 2.2).

If this model represented reality then it would explain a rise in
savings but not, without further assumptions, a rise in investment.
First, one would have to assume that savings were made available
for investment and not hoarded. If they were hoarded then the
result would simply be the abstraction of money from the economy
and a decline in either prices or economic activity. Profit opportunities through innovation could have provided the incentive for
higher levels of investment. This assumes that two different things –
a rise in saving and an increase in profit opportunities – came
together. This is quite possible, but there may be other ways of
modelling investment and its relationship with saving which eliminate coincidence.

One alternative is the orthodox neo-classical approach. 'Neo-
classical' covers a wide variety of economic analysis, but a fundamental position is that economic relationships tend towards an
equilibrium in which supply – of goods, labour or money – is
equated with demand through price. The assumption is that factors
of production are normally fully employed; if they are not, through
some temporary disequilibrium in demand or supply, then factor

prices will rise or fall as appropriate to restore equilibrium. Neo-classical analysis is therefore antithetical to the Lewis view in which labour may be in long-run surplus, and the Keynesian view in which both capital and labour are potentially in long-run surplus.

In the neo-classical view, existing savings constitute the supply of loanable funds, and the desire to invest constitutes the demand for such funds. If the desire to invest remains the same, increased savings will result in an increased supply of money and therefore a decrease in the price at which it can be borrowed. This price is the interest rate. There is not necessarily any more demand for investment, because of Schumpeterian innovation or anything else, but more investment will take place because the interest rate decline makes it cheaper. Projects which were marginal or uneconomic now become worth carrying out. So in the neo-classical model, increased savings drive investment. (Of course, declining interest rates will then reduce the incentive to save; but if incomes continue to increase and the marginal propensity to save is high, savings can still go up, as shown in Figure 2.2.) T.S. Ashton, a leading historian of the Industrial Revolution, saw a decline in the rate of interest as crucial to increased investment. This approach is not only compatible with the model of gradual accumulation sketched above, but actually depends on it.

Another alternative is the Keynesian approach, which will be discussed further in Chapter 4. Keynes attached less importance to the rate of interest as a factor in investment decisions, and on these assumptions a fall in interest rates would not have the impact Ashton attributed to it. So assuming the original savings rise as set out above, Keynesians would argue that there would at some stage have to be a greater desire to invest. Otherwise the saving would turn into hoarding, economic activity and incomes would decline and savings would fall again. In an analysis of the Industrial Revolution based on Keynesian assumptions, there might be various forces, apart from innovation, driving the increased desire to invest: an increase in population which increased demand, an increase in exports, or increased demand from government spending, which in the eighteenth century meant spending on war. Of course, none of these is directly connected with the slow growth of incomes which, it was postulated, drove the original rise in savings. To that extent a Keynesian approach also relies on coincidence. However, once a further growth in incomes takes

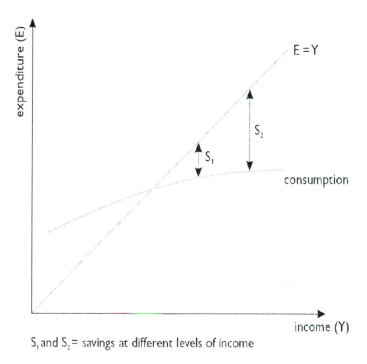

S_1 and S_2 = savings at different levels of income

Figure 2.2 Income and savings

place, as the increased investment produces more goods, then in a Keynesian world the higher incomes would produce the higher savings needed to finance further investment, and coincidence would be abolished.

So some models assume that savings were accumulated gradually, while others such as Lewis's assume that capitalists' savings initiated growth. What did eighteenth- and early nineteenth-century savers actually do?

Savers

The discussion below will largely focus on non-agricultural savers. Agriculturalists' saving was used for non-agricultural purposes, and to that extent will be mentioned. But most agricultural saving was likely to have gone into agricultural investment, which is not our concern.

Savers will be classed under three headings, the first being London savers. All the available evidence suggests that, outside agriculture, London was the principal generator of savings at the beginning of the eighteenth century and remained very important. This is what we would expect, because London was by far the largest and wealthiest city in the kingdom and should therefore have generated a high proportion of savings, particularly on the model outlined earlier in which savings rise faster than incomes. London savings came from disparate sources. The savings of the aristocracy and wealthier landed gentry, many of whom spent part of the year in London, were largely agricultural in origin. The savings of large merchants engaged in overseas trade, import or export, and of large manufacturers such as brewers, could be described, using Lewis's terminology, as capitalist. The savings of shopkeepers, small manufacturers – London had many luxury trades – and professional people could be described as middle-class.

While much of these savings would have been ploughed back into the savers' own businesses, or gone into house mortgages, a large proportion of London savings went into the Funds, especially government stocks. The wars of the late seventeenth and early eighteenth centuries were partially financed by the issue of such stocks. The government's total borrowings then declined gently until the mid-1740s when war expenditure pushed them up again, and from then on the succession of major wars in which Britain participated continued to drive the total ever higher. Most of these stocks were held in London or the London area; 87 per cent of the holders of one government stock between 1780 and 1793 came from London and its immediately adjoining counties.

London savers therefore financed a large proportion of Britain's wars as well as their own, very important, commercial activities. How much of their money went elsewhere? London merchants provided credit for a large proportion of the country's export trades, both those which went through London and trade elsewhere. Merchants, particularly the warehousemen (wholesalers), financed this with their own money and by issuing bonds which attracted small savers. Some found their financing activities so lucrative that they became bankers. On the other hand, much of the capital for other important developments did not come from London.

Finance for the early transport improvements came mainly from the next category, provincial savers. This includes everyone in Britain, outside London, who would fall into the middle-class category, and agriculturalists when their savings went into trade or industry. In the early eighteenth century it seems likely that the middle classes simply did not have the wherewithal to save much. So far as they did have surplus cash, it would be used mainly to finance their own commercial activities. As incomes and savings rose, some additional surplus became available. This could have been used to buy government stock, since the market for it was national even if the holders were mainly London-based; but as the wars of the early eighteenth century wound down and government issues dried up, the yield on its stocks fell sharply, fluctuating between 3 and 4 per cent from the late 1720s through to the 1770s. We can conjecture that existing London savers, lacking other outlets for their savings, were bidding up its price.

For provincial savers, turnpikes and canals offered a better yield. Turnpikes paid a fairly steady 5 per cent throughout this period, with limited reductions when the interest on government stocks was particularly low. Early trusts were financed mainly by a few wealthy local citizens. From 1750, as the boom in trusts got under way, the subscribers came from a much wider background. They included clerks, weavers, shoemakers, hairdressers – the small-town citizens who were the bedrock of provincial Britain in the mid-eighteenth century. Among the better-off subscribers, who still provided the bulk of the capital, were wealthier urban groups such as brewers and clothiers, but particularly landowners and farmers. So turnpikes attracted both urban and rural savers, with the latter probably being more important.

Canals, too, drew largely upon provincial savings. J.R. Ward has analysed the source of about one-third of the original subscriptions. In the earlier canals, built between 1755 and 1780, around 50 per cent of the subscriptions were by those connected with agriculture. By 1780–1815, encompassing the period of the great canal boom, the urban proportion went up to around 70 per cent. (In these figures, based on Ward's, clergymen, whose income was most likely to come from tithes on agricultural land, were counted in the agriculture category; female subscribers, three-quarters of whom lived in towns, were counted as urban.) Whether rural or urban in origin, the great majority of the investors came from the area of the canal in question. This was partly because, when canals were promoted, preference was often given to local shareholders. But, of course, this was only possible because the local shareholders were ready and willing to subscribe.

Increased provincial savings were not just going into turnpikes and canals. As described earlier, by the late eighteenth century large amounts of money were being lent on mortgage to merchants and manufacturers in Lancashire and Yorkshire, while increasing amounts were being deposited in banks. There was also the increasing flow of savings from agricultural areas which financed circulating capital in industrial areas. In addition, the growing numbers of houses being built outside London must have been largely financed from provincial sources, as house-mortgages were a local market until much later.

A third group of potential savers were capitalists, using the word in Lewis's sense to mean forward-looking businessmen with a strong drive to invest for profit. Their savings have already been mentioned within the categories above but it is worth focusing on them more closely because of their importance in models such as Marx's and Lewis's.

Much of their saving was ploughed back into their own firms; but as has already been noted, once these were established the owners were willing to move their capital elsewhere. In some industries, which were already mature early in the Industrial Revolution, this process began early. Thus in trades and industries dealing with agricultural products – hop merchanting, brewing, malting and the textile trades, for instance – established firms with surplus capital moved it into banking and thus, indirectly, into other trades and industries. In areas where there was rapid growth, capital often moved into related industries in which there were opportunities: the involvement in early textile manufacturing of cloth merchants and others in related trades is the classic example. By the late eighteenth and early nineteenth centuries some of these newer industries had begun to mature and allow firms in them to throw off cash and diversify. Capitalists also supported transport undertakings: in industrialising areas such as Lancashire they were big subscribers to turnpikes, although it seems likely that, overall, agriculture provided most money to that sector of transport; canals drew more on non-agricultural money. Using Ward's figures, merchants, bankers and manufacturers in dynamic industries such as cotton, iron and pottery can be separated out from the rest of the middle classes. All these groups together contributed over 20 per cent of the capital to the earlier canals built up to 1780, and 35 per cent to the more important group built 1780–1815. The latter figure suggests that, in spite of the numerous calls on capitalists' money, they still generated enough cash to invest substantially in canals. Furthermore these figures may understate the share of capitalists. The aristocracy and landowners, who together contributed about one-quarter of the capital of all canals up to 1815, would have included many whose income came in part from mining royalties or urban housing, and some whose family had made its wealth in trade or industry in the recent past and with it had bought an estate.

There is, potentially, another method of finding money for investment apart from savings, and that is through credit creation.

The usual objection to credit creation as a means of increasing investment is that it has pernicious side effects. If an investment is financed by credit, then resources such as labour which would have been engaged in producing food or consumer goods are set to work on the investment. The production of these commodities falls while the amount of money in circulation rises. The result of more money chasing fewer resources is rising prices. If money incomes are presumed to be stable, then living standards will fall. In effect, the investment will have been financed by those whose living standards have fallen: they will have made a forced saving. If those affected are determined to maintain their living standards, then they will attempt to raise their incomes and inflation or social dislocation, or both, will follow. In the long run, of course, the capital assets that have been created will produce additional goods or services, and everyone should be better off. Schumpeter did not worry about credit creation for that reason. He accepted that it would cause some inflation in the short term but argued that, once the boom started by the initial investment had worked its way through, the extra production flowing from the capital assets would depress prices. Inflation would be followed by deflation, and long-term price levels would not necessarily rise.

In practice we can also observe that, in the early stages of the

Industrial Revolution, industry was quite small-scale, so that even Schumpeterian investment booms would not absorb large quantities of resources. Whether or not labour was in surplus, the effect of additional credit-financed investment on inflation cannot have been large and would have been swamped by the similar effects produced by war.

Models and capital accumulation

Because there are no figures to tell us the origin of savings throughout the entire economy, it will not be possible to make definitive judgments on the models' predictions about saving. However, the evidence does give some clear indications and it is also possible to say something about investment.

In the standard neo-classical model advanced by Ashton, the growth of investment occurred as a result of a decline in interest rates. However, studies of both turnpikes and canals suggest that the best explanation of their rapid development from 1750 on is as a response to trade growth and the consequent likelihood of remunerative traffic levels. Invention can be ruled out as an explanation of the timing of their growth, because the principles of each were understood well before 1750. The interest rate was not a significant factor as turnpike loans paid, for the most part, a steady 5 per cent, while canals usually expected to earn more than this on their capital, although they did not always succeed. The other half of the neo-classical equation, the growth of savings, does appear to hold for both turnpikes and canals, which were financed from provincial savings which simply did not exist earlier on. But the simultaneous appearance of savings and investment opportunities was not just a happy coincidence; the slow and steady growth in the economy in the earlier eighteenth century had increased both incomes – and therefore, we conjecture, savings – and traffic levels.

In spite of this evidence, Larry Neal has argued that London interest rates did have a national applicability because they were reflected in the rates paid on government bonds which were available over the whole country. High interest rates would increase the attractions of bonds to businessmen and thus reduce investment in capital assets. In theory this effect would be exacerbated by the Usury Laws, a relic of an older way of thinking, which restricted interest on loans to 5 per cent; logically, loans would dry up when interest rates exceeded 5 per cent because bonds (whose price, and therefore the interest rate payable, fluctuated) were more attractive.

In practice, however, businessmen with money to lend could evade the Usury Laws at times of high interest rates by increasing the discount they allowed for prompt payment of debts, thus effectively raising the interest rate on the credit they extended. Thus surplus cash would not automatically flow into bonds and, although local short-term interest rates might rise in line with national rates, credit would not dry up. Furthermore medium- and long-term credit in the provinces was much less affected by national rates: the interest on the money advanced on mortgages to finance a variety of developments – the building of houses, the financing of industry in Lancashire and Yorkshire – tended to remain at 5 per cent even when national interest rates were higher. Here the force of custom and unfamiliarity with government bonds seems to have kept many savers to their familiar lending patterns. During the Napoleonic Wars, a period of consistently high rates, the investment ratio actually rose. If some savings were diverted from industrial investment because of the availability of higher rates elsewhere, this was presumably offset by greater plough-back. The Usury Laws were repealed in 1832, so the problem, if there was one, was mitigated. However, the evidence suggests that throughout the period there was much less impact on industrial investment from changing London rates than Neal suggests.

If businessmen were willing to invest without much reference to interest rates, this would fit in with any of the Lewis/Rostow/ Schumpeter models of capital accumulation. In all these models profits in modern capitalist industries are assumed to be high, so whether the interest rate fluctuated or was stable at around 5 per cent would not make much difference to businessmen. What does the evidence on saving tell us about these models?

Some money flowed into transport projects and into industry from agriculture, via subscription to loans and shares and the banking system. So agriculture was a source of savings for the British Industrial Revolution although neglected in Lewis's basic model. Agriculture generated savings in Britain because most agriculture was not peasant and subsistence, but capitalistic and effi- cient: some of the efficiency gain went to farmers who were themselves capitalists, albeit on a small scale, and were therefore likely to save; some went to landowners, most of whom also saved. Lewis thought that the middle classes would not save appreciably more over time, and were never likely to save much anyway. The evidence suggests that, for Britain, this is too pessimistic. As time went by the subscribers to turnpikes came from a wider social group than formerly, while advances on mortgage also originated from a wide range of people. The hardest evidence comes from canal subscriptions. Omitting the groups classed earlier as capitalist, the remaining non-agricultural groups – professional men, tradesmen, and women – subscribed 29 per cent of the capital of the earlier canals and 35 per cent of the capital of the later ones. These figures are impressive but they are not resoundingly so, for by the later period the group we classed as capitalists was investing as much as the middle classes, even though capitalists had a far wider range of uses for their money, notably in their own trades and industries. So the figures do suggest clear limits on the middle class's ability to finance industrialisation, and to that extent Lewis was right.

Elise Brezis has put forward a model in which savings came in part from abroad, pointing out that this is usual for a developing country, which Britain was in the eighteenth century. Most historians accept some role for Dutch savings, which at this period exceeded Dutch demand for investment; Brezis argues that they constituted a substantial proportion of savings. This contention depends on the accuracy of figures which are calculated from the residual differences between various problematical statistics, such as those for exports and imports. In other words, there is quite a high likelihood that the figures are wrong. Even if they are correct or on the right lines, Dutch money flowed into government stocks and a few internationally traded securities, and there is no evidence that it financed investment in fixed assets in industry and transport. It could only affect investment in these via interest rates, which it was suggested earlier were not of key importance.

An opposite argument is that savings were potentially in surplus. Savings were always available when they were necessary to finance wars; from the 1780s on the savings ratio in time of war rose to over 15 per cent. If these savings were potentially available for investment in peacetime, but for some reason were not used, it would appear to undermine Lewis's model. There are, however, counter-arguments. Lewis accepted that there might have been a wealthy segment in the population before industrialisation, but argued that they chose not to save their wealth but to spend it. Obviously eighteenth-century Britain was more complex, in that mechanisms for saving were well developed, and few wealthy people spent all their money in conspicuous consumption. But it does seem that many London savers, who purchased the bulk of government stocks which financed wars, were reluctant, like the Dutch, to place their savings in unfamiliar securities; so most investment outside London had to be financed locally, irrespective of fluctuations in the national savings ratio.

Equally important, the high savings ratio in time of war may have been caused in part not by high interest rates calling forth latent savings but by windfall gains for London savers. Among these were wealthy landowners, classed earlier as 'London savers', who gained because agricultural prices rose sharply, particularly during the Napoleonic Wars. Wealthy farmers would also gain, and by the turn of the century they would often place their spare cash in banks from which it was transmitted, via the London money market, to investors elsewhere, or placed in government stock. Another group who gained were wealthy merchants and bankers who made large profits from government contracts during wartime, from arranging the payment of troops overseas, and other war-related activities. One such was Richard Oswald, a great London trader with the Chesapeake in North America. Oswald made a fortune supplying bread to troops in the Seven Years' War, and then placed £100,000 of his profits in the Funds, a type of action which was probably quite common.

All this suggests that, while Britain had a high potential level of savings, these did not necessarily go into industry. To that extent Lewis's ideas have not been refuted, and saving by a particular group of capitalists engaged in modern industry may still have been important for further industrial development. On the other hand, it is clear that there were other significant sources of finance for industrialisation.

In some famous passages Marx spoke of a period of 'primitive accumulation' in which capital was amassed by colonial plunder, the slave trade and the concentration of land in the hands of a few. Obviously the first two did make a contribution to the capital available, although much of the profit gained from these sources went on extravagant houses and other luxury expenditure. Patrick

O'Brien has demonstrated that all trade with countries outside Europe – not just the slave trade – was highly unlikely to have contributed more than 7 per cent of total investment between the 1780s and the 1820s, and this is making generous assumptions regarding the rate of profit and the amount reinvested. Marx was on firmer ground in pointing to the importance of agricultural capital, but it was not all concentrated in the hands of great land-owners: farmers often had quite substantial sums while agricultural wealth helped to boost the prosperity of market towns and hence of the large group we have described as 'middle-class savers'. The distribution of wealth was highly unequal, of course. But most capital, at least going back to the recent past, was acquired through legitimate activity rather than by force or rapine.

Nothing in Schumpeter's approach, or in modern growth theories whether exogenous or endogenous, has been invalidated by the discussion so far. Their focus is on innovations as providing profit opportunities which encouraged investment, and certainly the investment ratio rose in the late eighteenth century as innovation accelerated. Their view that savings followed investment has neither been proved nor disproved: the provincial savings which flowed into turnpikes and mortgages seem to have been new, but on the other hand, the demand for investment seems to have been the crucial variable in its timing, not the supply of savings. Following from that, a demand-side explanation of growth is also still intact. The fact that savings seem to have been available in wartime is a support to a Keynesian interpretation. As noted above, however, there are caveats to the idea that this constituted a permanent surplus always potentially available for investment.

Table

Table 2.1 Investment

	I	II	III	
1700			4.0%	
1761–70	4.3	143	6.8%	(1760)
1781–90	7.0	188		
1801–10	20.1	649	8.5%	(1800)
1821–30	27.6	610		
1841–50	48.1	942	10.8%	(1840)

After Feinstein and Pollard, *Studies in Capital Formation*, Appendix, Table 1 (see further reading)

I   Annual average gross fixed capital formation (million pounds, current prices)
II   Net capital stock (i.e. after depreciation) at end of decade (million pounds, current prices)
III   Investment ratio (dates in parentheses)

Further reading

P. Hudson, *The Genesis of Industrial Capital: A Study of the West Riding Wool Textile Industry c. 1750–1850* (Cambridge, 1986), J.R. Ward, *The Finance of Canal Building in 18th-century England* (Oxford, 1974) and W. Albert, *The Turnpike Road System in England 1663–1840*, (Cambridge, 1972) are all valuable for the genesis of savings and the mechanism of investment; see also B.L. Anderson, 'Provincial aspects of the financial revolution of the 18th century', *Business History*, 11 (1969), pp. 11–22. C.H. Feinstein and S. Pollard, *Studies in Capital Formation in the United Kingdom, 1750–1920*, (Oxford, 1988) for investment by sector and overall. C.K. Harley, 'Reassessing the industrial revolution: a macro view', in J. Mokyr, *The British Industrial Revolution: An Economic Perspective* (Oxford, 1993) is very useful for a summary of recent statistical material on this and other subjects. J.F. Wright, 'British government borrowing in wartime 1750–1815', *EcHR*, 52 (1999), pp. 355–61 for a recent estimate of the savings ratio. See M.W. Kirby, *Men of Business and Politics* (1984) for Edward Pease; D. Brown, 'From "cotton lord" to landed aristocrat: the rise of Sir George Philips Bart., 1766–1847', *Historical Research*, 69 (1996), pp. 62–82 for George Philips; and D. Hancock, '"Domestic bubbling": eighteenth-century London merchants and individual investment in the Funds', *EcHR*, 47 (1994), pp. 679–702 for George Oswald.

T.S. Ashton, *An Economic History of England: The Eighteenth Century* (1955).

E.S. Brezis, 'Foreign capital flows in the century of Britain's industrial revolution: new estimates, controlled conjectures', *EcHR*, 48 (1995), pp. 46–67.

N.F.R. Crafts, 'The industrial revolution', in R. Floud and D. McCloskey, *The Economic History of Britain* (see Introduction).

L. Neal, 'The finance of business during the industrial revolution', in *ibid.*

L. Neal, *The Rise of Financial Capitalism: International Capital Markets in the Age of Reason* (Cambridge, 1990).

L.S. Pressnell, *Country Banking in the Industrial Revolution* (Oxford, 1956).

P.K. O'Brien, 'European economic development: the contribution of the periphery', *EcHR*, 35 (1982), pp. 1–18.

Chapter 3

Labour supply

'Unlimited supplies of labour'

Lewis suggested that unlimited supplies of labour kept wages down and allowed capitalists large profit margins, thus providing the finance for the increase in capital assets. There is not much evidence for this in the first half of the mid-eighteenth century: population was growing slowly, real wages were increasing, and finance came from agriculturalists and middle-class savers as well as large capitalists. However, in the mid-eighteenth century the investment ratio was around 6–7 per cent, while by 1840 it was much higher. So it remains quite possible that, over the intervening period, a Lewis-like effect on the supply price of labour was a vital component in Britain's ability to reach this rate of capital accumulation.

Given that labour was not obviously in surplus in the earlier eighteenth century, the most likely reason for a surplus to appear was through population growth. This hypothesis would suggest that, as population grew, there was not enough agricultural work for all the available workers, so rural wages were likely to be depressed or at least not rise. For a small wage advantage workers would move to towns; thus the supply price of urban labour would remain low as it depended on the rural wage. The model calls for labour to be mobile, and in Britain it was by comparison with Continental Europe, for by the eighteenth century much of Britain's agricultural population consisted of labourers with no ties to the land. The barriers to their migration were the cost of moving, the risk of moving away from known if ill-paid jobs and an existing network of contacts, and ignorance of alternative opportunities. For all these reasons most migration was short-distance, but it was substantial in volume even before industrialisation.

In spite of favourable conditions for the Lewis model to operate, there is a simple but fundamental problem with it when applied to late eighteenth- and early nineteenth-century Britain: in both money and real terms, rural wages were rising strongly in the north and Midlands where industrialisation was most rapid. The most likely reason for this was that the demand for male labour in the towns more than absorbed the surplus from rural areas in the locality, thus exerting an upward pressure on rural wages. Insofar as northern and Midland rural wages started at quite a low level, it may be that at first industrialists did benefit from cheap labour; but by the 1770s urban wages were rising in line with rural ones. Industrialising areas in the north and Midlands drew on their own population growth and that of adjacent rural areas, which was large but finite in relation to the growth of industry. The vast surplus population of southern agricultural areas, which might have provided labour to areas of industrialisation, did not do so because of the barriers to longer-distance migration outlined above. Instead, rural migrants from those areas mainly moved to southern towns and cities.

From the end of the Napoleonic Wars onwards, the northern and Midlands agricultural regions only slightly extended their wage lead over the south; real wages increased, but until 1850 the increase was slow and erratic. All this suggests that the growth in the demand for and supply of labour had reached an equilibrium. However, the investment ratio took one final leap upwards, from around 8 per cent during the wars to 11 per cent by 1840, leaving the possibility that a modified Lewis-type effect was at work. Modified, because the wages of northern agricultural labourers had risen well above subsistence level; but their subsequent stagnation is likely to have kept down urban workers' wages, so if productivity in industry had continued to rise, capitalists' profits would have increased. This effect may have been strengthened in various ways: by Irish immigration, by technological unemployment, by increases in hours worked and by the additional employment of women and children.

Irish immigration was high in the 1820s and 1830s and reached huge levels during the catastrophic potato famine of the 1840s. While many Irish went to London, the bulk of the migrants went to the north of England, particularly Lancashire, and the west of Scotland. Irish rural living standards were very low and so, potentially, was the supply price of Irish labour. On the other hand, it seems that as Irish immigration to British cities increased, the number of English migrants from rural areas declined. There would still have been some effect on urban wage levels, since the probable reason for this reduction was that Irish immigrants, who were prepared to accept very low wages, competed with English migrants for work. But there would have been no acceleration in the growth of the number seeking work, because increasing Irish immigration was countered by declining English migration. To that extent the extra supply of labour resulting from Irish immigration was limited.

Technological unemployment occurs when one technology rapidly replaces another and there are not enough appropriate new jobs to replace those lost from the old technology. In the 1820s and 1830s there was a rapid and large-scale shift as the powerloom was adopted for weaving, with the result that hand-loom weavers experienced extreme pressure on wage levels, such that for many the occupation became economically hopeless. Their numbers fell from around 250,000 in 1820 to 40,000 in 1850. As with Irish immigration, there are important caveats to the assumption that this necessarily increased labour supply. First, much of the resulting unemployment was in the textile areas of southwest England, notably Gloucestershire and Wiltshire, and was therefore unlikely to exert much downward pressure on wages in the Midlands and north. Second, the relative ease of learning the simpler kinds of hand-loom weaving meant that in the northwest it became the refuge of the most unskilled workers, which particularly meant Irish immigrants. Since the wage effect of such immigrants has already been discussed, adding in unemployed hand-loom weavers risks double-counting. And on the other side of the coin, the great bulk of powerloom weaving was in Lancashire and Yorkshire, so there was also a positive effect on labour demand in those areas.

It is possible that hours of work increased, and it has been suggested that factories were developed for this reason. The argument rests on the supposition that workers tended to enjoy the fruits of higher wages by taking more leisure, so the only way to extract more work effort was to introduce factories where workers were concentrated under the eye of the employer or an overseer. There is, however, plentiful evidence that factories developed because of technological imperatives. Early textile machinery was not built with the notion that it would be installed in a large, centralised, workplace. But it became apparent once Richard Arkwright's roller spinning machine was working that it could be used with waterpower and hence there was a technical reason for the factories which he built in the 1770s. (They were not the first – there had been large factories in the silk industry from 1719.)

While workers in factories did work more regular hours, in workshops and domestic industries workers seem to have continued with their old habits: they might take 'St. Monday' off at the beginning of the week but they then worked harder towards the end to make up. Hours of work increased substantially in late eighteenth-century London but this might have been due to particular London circumstances discussed in Chapter 4. Any general increase is unproven for the national economy, and the wage rise in the north and Midlands remains strong evidence that, in those areas, demand for male labour was increasing faster than supply up to the early nineteenth century. To the extent that the extra hours were worked by women and children, who were most affected by the discipline of the early factories, the subject is dealt with below.

Did the employment of women and children allow the modern capitalist sector to bypass wage rises elsewhere in the economy? Children's wages were notoriously low while women's wages were usually between one-third and two-thirds of men's. The rise in male wages would then be explained as a result of urban growth rather than direct industrial employment, urban growth providing all sorts of jobs outside modern industry, for instance in building, which were filled by men. However, well-paid men were not just employed in traditional sectors but predominated in most modern capitalist sectors. These included the iron industry, engineering and coalmining, the last of which employed around 50,000 workers in 1800 and over 100,000 by 1830. The most striking example is the Yorkshire woollen industry. Mills in this industry developed out of cooperative ventures by artisan clothiers and employment remained predominantly male. So among the rapidly-growing sectors cotton, which did employ large numbers of women and children, was the exception.

There is further evidence in Sarah Horrell's and Jane Humphries' study of women's and children's earnings throughout the British economy. This suggests that their contribution to family income, averaged from the 1780s to the 1840s, was around 25 per cent in miners' families, 20 per cent in skilled artisans', and 25–35 per cent in factory workers'. The contribution was even higher among low-paid outworkers, that is those working at home. While the children's income was likely to come from the same occupation as the father, the mother often worked at something different. In most cases, children's earnings predominated over women's by a large margin, not because children's wages were higher but because there were more of them. These figures suggest a substantial role for female and child labour, but as suggested above, not a dominant one. In modern industries, child labour – which included young men and women – was most prominent in cotton textiles. Even if other industries were not dependent on high profits from paying women and children low wages, it could be argued that cotton did rely on this for its profits and that these provided the wherewithal for the explosive growth of that industry, which was very important in its own right.

While female and child employment may have contributed to high profits in the cotton industry in the early period of factories from the 1780s to the 1800s, such employment was not unmitigated gain to the employer. Children were less productive than adults because of their lack of strength and stamina, because they needed more supervision and because of their lower skill levels: the last of these reflects the fact that expertise in textile occupations was built up over time. Children may have been paid a rate below the level their productivity warranted, but the gap may not have been substantial, and some would argue that it did not exist. If children's low wages largely reflected their low productivity, employers would not have received much benefit from paying these low wages. More controversially, Joyce Burnette has argued that lower female wages, in occupations shared with men, were also a reflection of lower productivity. This resulted from shorter hours of work, less physical strength and lower levels of human capital embodied in training. However, Burnette accepts that customary limitations on women's entry to many occupations may have over-crowded occupations largely staffed by women and depressed wages in these. Whether Burnette is right or wrong, there were other costs to low wages, such as high turnover of labour. Employers in a competitive market will bid for labour which is exceptionally cheap by paying higher wages; although the assumption of unlimited supplies of female and child labour puts a lid on the level which their wages will reach, there will still be a likelihood of high turnover as employers bid for workers who have acquired some training by offering marginal wage increments. As will be seen below, by the early nineteenth century cotton-factory owners were beginning to move away from a paradigm of low wages and high labour turnover to the opposite. If an alternative approach to labour management was considered economically feasible, the profits engendered by paying women and children relatively low wages could not have been that high.

Efficiency wages and human capital

From the 1780s to around 1820 most firms in cotton spinning alternated between preferences for male and female spinners, but by the latter date they had swung decisively towards the employment of men. Men were considered more effective supervisors and better able to cope with maintaining the long spinning mules which were being introduced. In reality, women may have been just as competent but that was not how employers saw it. The men were paid much higher wages than women, although in the 1820s employers still tried to keep wages down in times of depression. Since workers were paid according to output, or by the 'piece', wages were cut by reducing 'piece rates'. Workers responded by going slow, which reduced their earnings but also pushed up employers' overhead costs per unit of output. So from around 1830 firms in some of the biggest cotton towns moved towards paying what Michael Huberman calls 'fair wages'. This concept is a variation of efficiency wage theory, which assumes that it is worth paying workers above a market-clearing wage to elicit higher productivity, through more effort and less labour turnover: there will be a wage level 'A' at which the firm is best off, in that paying still higher wages would not extract commensurate extra productivity, and 'A' will therefore be the wage paid. Huberman suggests that simple efficiency wage theory does not address the issue that, in order to gain workers' full commitment, they need to perceive wages as fair and not liable to arbitrary change. This was achieved from 1829 by the introduction of wages for each town calculated by reference to standard 'lists', which took account of

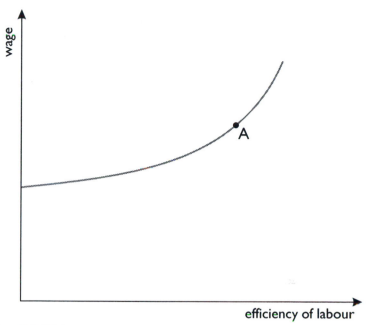

Figure 3.1 Efficiency wages

variables such as the quality of cotton. Both firms and workers benefitted, the latter through improved wage levels and because the new paradigm included a tacit acceptance that continuity of employment was the norm. The cotton industry had therefore come a long way in thirty years from the competitive labour market of around 1800, which is why Huberman entitled his book of 1996 *Escape from the Market*. Yet it was still economic to run spinning mills with these higher pay scales, and indeed the Lancashire cotton industry continued to grow rapidly. Paying the lowest wages possible had not provided the quality and consistency of work firms needed to keep expensive machinery running smoothly.

Efficiency wages are to do with eliciting effort and commitment. Wages might also be raised because workers embody human capital, in the form of skill and knowledge, which makes their labour more valuable. Human capital is potentially important to industrialisation in two ways. First, it enhances economic efficiency because workers are better trained, more literate and so forth, and therefore better at their jobs. Second, human capital enhances the ability of the economy both to generate and to make use of innovations. This is why endogenous growth theory sees it as so important. In practice these two aspects are hard to separate but analytically there is a clear distinction: the first is about increasing productivity in the same way that additions of physical capital increase it – by adding more of the same; the second is about facilitating change.

In the mid-eighteenth century perhaps two-thirds of men and 40 per cent of women were literate, and these figures had not changed much by 1840. In between, there may have been a dip until the early nineteenth century, followed by some revival, and the dip was probably as deep, or more so, in industrial areas as elsewhere. This ties in with what we know about schooling. In the late eighteenth century, the available provision was swamped by the rise in population; by the nineteenth century churches began to provide more educational facilities whilst parents themselves, at least in higher wage areas, were often willing to pay small amounts towards their children's education.

Whether or not the stagnation in literacy levels made much difference is not clear. Britain started with a fairly high level of literacy in relation to most Continental countries, and the actual number of people who needed to be literate in order to do their jobs properly was small, since even skilled manual work was for the most part done by eye or rule of thumb. But it was useful to have a wide pool from which those who did need literacy – merchants, clerks, surveyors and engineers, for instance – could be drawn, so that the quality of such people could be reasonably high. It has been suggested that, because of this need for some level of literacy, there was a critical level below which industrialisation could not have developed. However, there is general agreement that most countries in western Europe had reached that level, so Britain's relatively high literacy rate was unlikely to have been a significant influence on the broad thrust of industrialisation. On the other hand, Britain might still have been better off with a higher rate of literacy. Such 'might have beens', or to give them their technical name, counterfactuals, are highly speculative. They depend on assumptions, in this case that a higher rate of literacy would have increased individual earnings. In a mid-nineteenth-century sample of bridegrooms, the literate ones – literacy conventionally being measured by the ability to sign one's name – tended to have better-paid jobs than the illiterate. (The evidence is not clear for women.) Using these figures David Mitch has estimated that, by spending more on schooling, national income would have risen by between 2 and 7 per cent, the range being due to the uncertainties inherent in the exercise. As Mitch says, even the larger of these figures is not that great, although it is certainly not negligible. Assuming that this basic argument is correct, the failure to spend more on education can be seen as a market failure. In other words, a free market in education was not able to ensure an efficient allocation of resources. The probable reason for this was that, with a highly-skewed distribution of national income, many parents were unable to support their children through even a few years of education. Until the 1840s government funding to help such parents was minimal; after that date it increased, parents' incomes also rose, and literacy rates improved rapidly.

To a large extent the skills of manual workers were developed by on-the-job training, so the existence in mid-eighteenth-century Britain of a reasonable industrial base in industries such as shipbuilding, mining and iron-smelting was a valuable asset. In these industries skills were built up through long experience and were very difficult to transmit on paper. John Harris has shown how difficult the French found it to transfer skills from England, especially those which involved the use of coal. When the French imported English workers, language was a barrier to the oral transmission of knowledge, and to make matters worse, the English frequently got drunk. In both mining and iron-smelting, recruitment was usually from within existing families or communities, although at times of rapid expansion green labour was hired. It was difficult for employers to break this familial recruitment even if they had wished to, because they were reliant on the skills of the workers. In practice employers accepted it because it provided a cheap mechanism for the transmission of skills to new workers. For workers such as miners and iron-smelters, these skills were not so much ones of manual dexterity, although obviously that and strength were needed, but rather of judgment. A miner, for example, needed to know how to effectively cut coal from the face and be able to judge different grades of coal. A youngster could acquire these skills whilst working at various jobs in the mine, such

as driving the ponies which hauled coal along the main under-
ground passages or 'putting' – the manual haulage of coal from the
face to these passageways.

In all these cases, a smaller inheritance of human capital would
have placed barriers in the way of growth. There would have had to
be either formal training schemes – costly and unlikely to have
worked well in view of the tacit nature of the skills – or a much
greater utilisation of green labour, which would have been less
productive. In the case of coal-using industries such as those
involving the smelting of metals, Britain's early start gave it a formi-
dable advantage.

For the transmission of skills in a number of occupations which
involved both observation and extensive practice, there was a
reasonably effective institutional arrangement: this was apprenticeship. Originally both a statutory and customary practice for
ensuring that youngsters were trained and socialised – pre-industrial apprentices lived with their masters or mistresses – it ceased to
be statutory but nonetheless continued in unchanging trades such
as those in the building industry, as well as spreading into engineering and small but vital occupations such as instrument-making.
Living-in apprenticeship, however, declined and most apprentices
lived with their parents. Apprenticeship provided a mechanism by
which youngsters – overwhelmingly boys in the trades mentioned
above, although there were female apprentices in, for instance,
dress-making – received training and also a wage. The latter was
important because it ensured that working-class parents,
dependent as they were on their children's earnings, could afford to
apprentice their children. Even so, it tended to be better-off workers
who could afford it, since apprentices' wages were usually lower
than those of non-apprentices of the same age.

Apprenticeships usually lasted from around four to as many as
seven years, and in the first two a boy would do little work of
economic value but would observe and practise. This imposed a
cost on the employer, which in some cases was recouped by
charging a premium when an apprentice started. This practice
declined, however, and usually the employer's initial cost was
recouped in the later years of apprenticeship, when the adolescent
or young man was virtually capable of doing a skilled man's job but
was paid a lower wage. The sanctions on an apprentice leaving
early and moving elsewhere for higher wages were practical rather

than legal. An early leaver would not receive his apprentice 'lines' showing completion, and without these respectable employers would not employ men on skilled work. Unions also opposed the earning of skilled wages by men who had not served a full apprenticeship.

Apprenticeship was subject to many abuses. There were, for instance, pauper apprentices who served at low wages in isolated country cotton mills and learned little of value. Even in so-called skilled apprenticeship there was often exploitation. For instance, apprentices would be put on barely-skilled repetitive production which impeded their learning. However, in industries where apprenticeship conferred no advantage on young workers and merely provided employers with cheap labour, it quickly broke down since children and parents could easily see through it. Pauper apprentices, who had no autonomy, were a tragic but small minority. So, broadly speaking, apprenticeship served as a reasonably effective and cheap means of transmitting and increasing human capital.

Even for less-skilled workers there were similar forces at work. H.M. Boot has shown that in textile mills in the 1830s, children received a lower wage than they could have gained outside. Boot attributes this not to the payment of wages at a level below average productivity, since as suggested above most children, or their parents, had a degree of choice and did not have to accept excessively low wages. It was rather that the children lacked skill since, as with apprenticeship, this took time to accumulate by on-the-job training. In a textile mill some productive work could be done immediately, however, so children earned their wage from the beginning; consequently the institutional mechanism which apprenticeship provided for discouraging early leaving was not necessary.

In contrast to the children's wages, adult textile workers' earnings were much higher than those of unskilled workers, and Boot attributes this to the skilled nature of the work. This is compatible with Huberman's analysis in which wages also reflect effort and commitment, since the commitment of Huberman's workers was valuable precisely because they also exercised skill. If skill had not been necessary for textile work, paying efficiency wages would have had limited advantages. Boot estimates that the wages that boys in textile mills sacrificed, compared with boys doing unskilled work, amounted to £5 or so by the age of fifteen. The annual average expenditure on education per child in the 1830s has been estimated at about one pound and five shillings (£1.25), which suggests that, even for non-apprenticed children, training costs were significant in relation to the total cost of education.

The early accumulation of skills in Britain, and on-the-job training through formal apprenticeship or in factory work, all contributed to human capital formation. The use made of human capital was at the root of Adam Smith's dictum that the growth of the market enabled greater specialisation, or in his words 'division of labour'. Smith's famous example was pin-making, in which division into eighteen separate stages increased workers' productivity by at least two hundred and forty times. One suspects that Smith exaggerated but his point is clear. Specialisation increased the productivity of training, and therefore the productivity of human capital which embodied training. Instead of it taking years to train an all-round worker, a detail worker acquired sufficient skill in a few weeks or months and still worked much faster. Marx elaborated Smith's idea into one component of his own growth model, which also became part of his critique of capitalism. He accepted that increasing specialisation decreased the cost of training, or in his words 'reproducing', labour. He then argued that this made possible a reduction in wages. By implication this encouraged higher profits and therefore capital investment.

Marx's argument has some credence in that industrialists and inventors were sometimes explicitly concerned with simplifying tasks in order to replace skilled labour with unskilled. The classic example is the search for an improved self-acting mule, which was prompted, according to Richard Roberts the inventor, by employers anxious to undermine the skilled mule-spinners. However, there is little evidence that, over the economy as a whole, things worked as Marx thought. He believed that 'machinofacture' – by which he meant the use of machines in production – involved even less skill than subdivided 'manufacture' – by which he meant handwork, although it has come to mean all types of production. This belief was one of his big mistakes. While tending simple machines involved little skill, many machines were complex; but it was not economic to have one person to carry out each task, so machine operators carried out more tasks than the average detail hand-worker. A spinning-mule operator, for example, had to carry out a number of complex tasks involving skill and judgment.

In other industries, subdivision did take place. However, this occurred not as a deliberate attempt to economise on training, but as a necessity if higher quality and greater sophistication were to be achieved. Thus an entire waterwheel and its machinery might have been built and installed by a millwright and unskilled helpers. A steam engine, however, would need pattern-makers, blacksmiths and turners to shape the parts and fitters to put them together. The skill of each individual might be comparable to that of the mill-wright, but the total skill content of the finished product was much greater – just as the skill content of a modern product such as a jet turbine is far greater than that of a steam engine.

Both Marx's and Smith's insights into the division of labour therefore contain some truth but do not tell the whole story. Over the whole economy, the skill needed was constantly increasing as products became more sophisticated. The expense of training would have increased commensurately unless work had become more subdivided. However, this division of labour did not always take the simple form of Smith's pin-making example; instead, specialisation often enabled workers to develop their skills to a much higher level. Of course, the skills needed for a particular task did not always increase and so Marx was in part correct in suggesting that capitalists subdivided work to reduce training costs. However, this was only one of many influences on the arrangement of work among workers, and there is no evidence of a unilateral tendency towards an overall reduction in skill, or 'de-skilling'.

Can we get beyond such broad-brush generalisations to assess the importance of the additions to the total stock of skills and literacy? Unfortunately, there are no reliable estimates as to their magnitude. Boot has suggested that investment in training, in the form of foregone wages, equalled investment in formal education in the 1830s. He cites West's estimate that the latter amounted to 10 per cent of fixed capital formation, which suggests that education and training together were 20 per cent of the latter. However, Boot's figures apply to factory workers only; training costs would have been higher for most apprenticed workers but lower for the many unskilled workers. Also, training and education investments in earlier years would have been different, although not necessarily lower in relation to fixed capital formation; as a result, 20 per cent cannot be taken as a reliable figure. Another complication is that workers whose skills were replaced by machines had these skills rendered valueless. They were relatively few in number, but the reduction in their wages, which reflected the obsolescence of their personal human capital, should nonetheless form part of any calculation of the value of human capital in the economy as a whole.

Whatever the total increase in human capital, the increasing efficiency of training because of the division of labour should be remembered. Without this, efficiency gain training would have been more expensive and, most likely, less would have been undertaken. But assessing the extent of the gain is likely to be even more difficult than assessing the cost of the training itself.

Since it is so difficult to assess the investment in and productivity of training, it might be better to examine its results. In spite of the relative cheapness of on-the-job training – its main cost being foregone wages – there was probably not as much taking place as would have been economically ideal. Boot has suggested that the enhanced earnings of textile workers offered very high returns on their original investment of foregone wages; high returns were also available to apprenticeship, judging by the differential between skilled and unskilled wages. If there had been more training, skilled wages would have fallen because of the greater supply of skilled workers; total wage income would not necessarily have fallen, however, as more workers would have earned a higher level of wages. Since costs and therefore prices would have fallen, the economy would have been better off.

Why was there not more training, given the long-term rewards to individual workers? One argument is that trade-union rules limited the number of apprentices, in order to keep skilled wages artificially high. But there is no evidence that unions were strong enough in this early period to have any such effect, except perhaps in a few craft trades in London. It is much more likely that, as with literacy, market failure prevented higher investment in training. Girls' training was sharply constrained, probably mainly by prejudice although there may have been uncertainties as to the length of girls' working careers which led to less desire to invest in training. Large numbers of rural adolescents could not train in industrial skills, because the opportunities to do so were only available to youngsters in towns. Finally, many of the urban poor were unlikely to use these opportunities for their own children. This was due partly, no doubt, to ignorance as to wages and job prospects outside their immediate horizons; partly to uncertainty about the future; and partly to the fact that poverty led them to put a very high value on their children's present earnings. Therefore they would not pay for formal education or accept the sacrifice of lower wages for occupations which involved training. Instead, they tended to set their children to occupations which paid the highest wages irrespective of the prospects.

So some further investment in training would have been useful to the economy. On the other hand, Britain clearly gained because the prior accumulation of skills, and the early development of division of labour and the factory system, meant that it could be economic to train large numbers of workers, even if this number was not the optimum. As an addition to, or substitute for, physical capital, this must have made some difference to the rate of industrialisation. However, international comparison suggests that industrialisation is possible with a fairly low skills base. When the USA industrialised rapidly in the later nineteenth century, it had a high proportion of unskilled migrant and rural labour, so industrialists economised on the use of skill by introducing more specialised machinery. Obviously some skilled workers are necessary as some work cannot be broken down into less-skilled components – iron-making, already mentioned, is an example – but the number might not be that high.

Even if we could estimate how much human capital formation there was, the answer, or the fact that the amount was probably less than optimum, probably does not matter all that much. A certain amount more or less of skill formation, or even some reduction in its efficiency, would have made some difference to growth but not a great deal. However, the existence of skills in certain industries at the beginning of the Industrial Revolution may have been important. But if so, it was important not because these skills constituted a certain measurable quantity of human capital, but because they were part of the environment which endogenous growth theorists see as facilitating innovation. And this is a subject for discussion later, in Chapter 5.

Marx, Lewis, and the supply of labour

Apart from believing that de-skilling lowered wages, Marx thought that wages were kept down by technological unemployment, which created in his parlance a 'reserve army of labour', or in other words a labour surplus. The similarity with Lewis is only superficial, the latter specifically rejecting technological unemployment as a cause of surplus. In contrast, Marx thought technological unemployment was not just a one-off occurrence such as was experienced by the handloom weavers, but was a permanent feature of capitalism, as innovations constantly destroyed old ways of doing things.

There are both empirical and theoretical objections to this picture. There was always a large number of semi-employed labourers in both countryside and towns, especially in the south, but this was a consequence of the Lewis-like rural surplus, exacerbated by population increase. Superimposed on this were periods such as the post-Napoleonic War years and the early 1840s, when severe depressions led to widespread unemployment; but this was cyclical rather than technological. Most industries undergoing rapid innovation employed increasing numbers of workers. This occurred because in these industries growth was fast enough to create more jobs, in spite of labour-saving innovations. Even in modernising industries, older technologies were usually replaced gradually, as, for instance, when steam replaced water power, a process which was still underway in the mid-nineteenth century. The effect on labour of such gradual replacement was likely to be minimal, as the labour force of the older technology continued in work while a younger generation of workers supplied the labour force for the new technology. Rapid but small-scale technological changes sometimes threw small groups of workers out of employment but had little effect on the total labour supply. The unemployment of the handloom weavers, in which change was large-scale, rapid and not accompanied by the simultaneous development of as many new jobs, was unique.

Proto-industrialisation theory sees capitalists utilising cheap labour in the countryside to reduce the cost of textile production. This undoubtedly happened, and was one reason for the early eighteenth-century expansion of woollen textiles in the West Riding of Yorkshire and the hosiery industry in the East Midlands. It was not new, since merchants had been seeking to cheapen costs in this way in many parts of western Europe since the sixteenth century. Although the theory does not assume that capitalists used the latest techniques of production, and in that sense is different from Lewis's, there are similarities in the suggestion that the superprofits from proto-industrialisation were invested in the early factories. As the evidence reviewed in Chapter 2 suggests, however, capital in Britain was available from many sources: agriculture, wealthy merchants engaging in foreign trade, urban tradesmen, brewers and many others. No doubt merchants engaged in domestic industry, as proto-industrialisation used to be called, made a contribution but there is no evidence that it was more than a tributary of the river of capital which existed anyway. Proto-industrialisation theory has nothing to say about technical innovation – if anything, the use of relatively cheap labour would have discouraged the use of labour-saving machinery.

Proto-industrialisation theory can be seen as a variant of Lewis's model, but one in which the function of labour surplus is limited to enabling cheap textile production in rural areas. Because of this the superprofits envisaged are themselves limited and cannot bear the weight the theory would like to place on them. What of Lewis's original model? This provides a much more complete explanation, since it sees capitalists in any industry, and in town and country, as potential users of cheap labour. While the payment of efficiency wages and the existence of wage premia for skill are complications, they do not necessarily invalidate the model. Surplus labour, even if it was initially unskilled, would act as a reservoir which would keep all wages down unless a group of workers could totally segment themselves from the rest of the labour market. However, the wide-spread existence of various kinds of wage differential undoubtedly weakens Lewis's argument; in many cases, these differentials were supported by partial labour market segmentation so competition from other workers was limited. Skill premia, for example, were largely paid to men, because women were excluded from many skilled occupations, and thus the female labour surplus was more or less irrelevant to skilled wages. In theory employers could still replace expensive men with cheap women, but only if the technology concerned could easily shift from a high skill to a low skill input. In the case of many industries this was likely to be uneconomic: employing fewer but more highly skilled-workers was cheaper. In the same sort of way, efficiency wages were largely paid to male factory workers, at least in the cotton industry. Once employers offered tacit employment guarantees to underpin efficiency wages, workers were in a position to form trade unions, which were more effective in spinning than in most early nineteenth-century industry. This made it difficult for employers to move back to the earlier low wage/high turnover regime.

The most cogent criticism of the Lewis model is that wages in modernising industries in the areas of most rapid industrial growth grew rapidly, if intermittently, during the period of industrialisation. The probable reason for this was that a high proportion of the largest single source of surplus labour, males who had been born in rural areas, were in the south of England and for the most part stayed there. In other words, limited inter-regional labour mobility mitigated the impact of the rural surplus. After the Napoleonic Wars, Irish immigration and technological unemployment may have had some effect in keeping down wage levels in the north, although not as much as is sometimes suggested.

The problem of capital accumulation is central to Lewis's model, but the suggested mechanism by which this took place – unlimited supplies of labour – does not seem to apply to British industrialisation, while in Britain the savings which flowed into industry were provided by a variety of sources, not just by capitalists. These comments do not, of course, necessarily invalidate the applicability of the model to industrialisation at other times and in other places.

Further reading

P.M. Solar, 'Poor relief and English economic development before the industrial revolution', *EcHR*, 48 (1995), pp. 1–22 outlines some of the reasons for high labour mobility; see also J.G. Williamson, *Coping with City Growth during the British Industrial Revolution* (Cambridge, 1990). For skills J. Harris, 'Skills, coal and British industry in the eighteenth century', *History*, 61 (1976), pp. 167–82 and *Industrial Espionage and Technology Transfer: Britain and France in the 18th Century* (Aldershot, 1998) are invaluable; see also H.M. Boot, 'How skilled were Lancashire cotton factory workers in 1833?', *EcHR*, 48 (1995), pp. 283–303 and J. Jaafe. *The Struggle for Market Power: Industrial Relations in the British Coal Industry 1800–1840* (Cambridge, 1991); C. More, *Skill and the English Working Class 1870–1914* (1980) has a chapter on the early history of apprenticeship. D. Mitch, 'The role of human capital in the first industrial revolution', in J. Mokyr, *The British Industrial Revolution: An Economic Perspective* (Oxford, 1993) is better on literacy than other forms of human capital. For women's work M. Berg, *Age of Manufactures* (see Introduction) and 'Women's work and the industrial revolution' in P. Sharpe, *Women's Work: The English Experience 1650–1914* (1998); D. Bythell, 'Women in the workforce', in P.K. O'Brien and R. Quinault, *The Industrial Revolution and British Society* (Cambridge, 1993); S. Horrell and J. Humphries, 'Women's labour force participation and the transition to the male breadwinner family, 1790–1865', *EcHR*, 48 (1995), pp. 89–117. For Marx on the division of labour and the reserve army of labour see *Capital*, vol. 1, pp. 339–57, 384 and 590–2 in the Lawrence and Wishart 1954 edition. S.R. Jones, 'Technology, transaction costs and the transition to factory production in the British silk industry 1700–1870', *JEH*, 47 (1987), pp. 71–96 deals succinctly with competing explanations for the setting-up of factories, concluding that technology, the obvious explanation, is also the correct one. For proto-industrialisation, versions of which aim to explain not just capital accumulation but also population growth, factories and other phenomena, see Clarkson, *Proto-industrialisation* (see Chapter 1) and D.C. Coleman, 'Proto-industrialisation: a concept too many', *EcHR*, 36 (1983), pp. 435–48; in recent years interest in the idea has lessened.

J. Burnette, 'An investigation of the female-male wage gap during the industrial revolution in Britain', *EcHR*, 50 (1997), pp. 257–81.

M. Huberman, *Escape from the Market: Negotiating Work in Lancashire* (Cambridge, 1996).

E.H. Hunt, *British Labour History 1815–1914* (1981).

E.H. Hunt, 'Industrialisation and regional inequality: wages in Britain 1760–1914', *JEH*, 46 (1986), pp. 935–66.

Chapter 4

Demand

Many accounts of the Industrial Revolution give demand-side forces an important role in stimulating growth. In practice the conditions under which such forces could act need to be carefully specified, and when this is done it is clear that they do not automatically produce the effects which are often attributed to them.

Suppose that the existing land, labour and capital of the country are fully employed. This being the case, on the assumptions of neo-classical economic theory the effect of additional demand, however it comes about, will not be to increase production but to either increase prices or shift output from one sector to another without it necessarily increasing in total. The reasoning behind this is simple: if the factors of production are fully employed, then whatever the demand they cannot produce more. When money supply increases as a result of increasing demand, the outlet is prices. The suggestion has often been made that, in the Industrial Revolution, rising prices became the stimulus, either to innovation, additional investment, or both. Again, given the original assumptions, this would not have happened. If all prices had risen at the same rate and simultaneously – as would occur if the demand was evenly spread – then there would not have been any additional stimulus to businessmen to economise in one way or another, for instance by developing machinery to displace labour. To put it another way, businessmen should have been looking for opportunities to economise anyway, whatever the demand conditions. Nor would there have been any possibilities of supernormal profits from rising prices which might have encouraged additional investment, since costs would have risen as fast as prices, and thus profit margins would have remained the same as before. In practice if interest rates for business borrowing were sticky, as suggested in the previous chapter, then that element of costs would have risen more slowly and there might have been some superprofits and some incentive to substitute capital for labour. But the constraints on the availability of capital and labour would still have existed: the failure of interest rates to increase would have hampered the expansion of credit, so investment would have been restricted. If the additional demand affected some sectors but not others, then as prices rose in those sectors resources would have shifted towards them. This may have given rise to some net increase in income, if, for instance, the growing sectors experienced economies of scale and the declining sectors did not. But there would still have been a decrease in output in other sectors, so the net output gain would have been limited.

Keynesian assumptions, however, provide a framework in which an increase in demand could affect growth in a much more dynamic way. They assume a situation in which labour is underemployed and the flow of savings is below its potential level at full employment. Extra demand, therefore, can be met and prices will not necessarily rise. Surplus labour will keep wages down, and so the higher profits from rising output will not be squeezed by rising wages. But total incomes will rise, both because of increased profits and because more people are at work. As incomes rise, so will spending, and the additional purchases will put more people to work, thus increasing incomes further and so on. These beneficial repercussions of an initial increase in incomes are known as 'the multiplier'. The rise in incomes will also increase savings and these savings will provide the wherewithal for further investment.

Unlike Lewis, who perceived a lack of capital in pre-industrial societies as their crucial problem, a Keynesian-type interpretation sees both capital and labour as potentially in surplus. The problem is a lack of demand to keep them occupied. Keynes himself saw growth before the First World War as a natural response to the discoveries of the New World and the flow of inventions, both of which increased profit opportunities, and did not think the issue was problematic. The assumption of this chapter is that other mechanisms which can be fitted into a Keynesian framework might have been brought into play, and therefore the further assumption that both capital and labour were in surplus will underpin the discussion. This will enable the possible impact of demand increases on growth to be explored within the most favourable scenario.

Population growth

The population of Britain rose from around 7.5 million in 1750 to over 20 million in 1850. One's intuitive conviction is that this increase must have caused demand to grow and that such growth must have had a major effect on industrialisation. However, for this hypothesis to be even a possibility, the population increase would have had to be independent of industrialisation. If the growth of industry itself caused all, or a large part, of the population increase, then logically population increase could not have been the initial cause of industrialisation.

The immediate causes of the increase – that is, whether it was caused by declining mortality, rising fertility or some combination of these – will be outlined before looking at the deeper reasons behind these changes. That will give a basis for assessing whether the population increase was independent of industrialisation.

While mortality declined, around 70 per cent of the rise in population from the early eighteenth to the mid-nineteenth century was due to a rise in fertility – the number of live births per woman – rather than a decline in mortality. Historical demographers can be very precise about why fertility rose. It rose partly because women married earlier, and to a lesser but significant extent because the interval between live births shortened. By the end of the 1820s women were marrying at an average age of around twenty-three as opposed to over twenty-five in the years before 1750, and these extra childbearing years came when women were most fertile. Furthermore, although the number of illegitimate births as a total of all births remained small, more women conceived before marriage so the age of first conception actually fell faster than the age of marriage.

What lay behind this falling age of marriage? One explanation is that it was caused by greater prosperity. The first half of the eighteenth century saw improving agricultural productivity, yet only a slow increase in population. As a result, real wages rose. This rise continued up to the late eighteenth century before real wages levelled out for a substantial period. This apparent equilibrium conceals regional variations, with real wages in the south falling while those in the north were more buoyant. The fall in the age of marriage was well under way in the years leading up to 1750, and continued after that date. Then in the early nineteenth century it

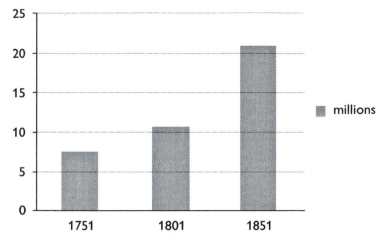

Figure 4.1 Population in Britain 1751–1851 (after Table 4.1)

started to rise again, returning almost to its 1750 level by 1850 before falling again. There are some coincidences between this and the changes in wages, but they are not great. In the first part of the period real wages did grow in line with the fall in the age of marriage; but in the years after 1820 they also grew, if uncertainly and unevenly, while the marriage age rose. Improvement in real wages can be more reliably connected with the reduction in the interval between live births. It seems highly likely that this was due to a reduction in the number of stillbirths, and that this reduction may have been caused by improving maternal health and nutrition. Such an improvement in women's health was likely to have gone right back to their childhood and even to that of their own mothers: healthy mothers had healthy babies who themselves became healthy mothers. So an improvement in nutrition would have a long-term impact which could carry over for several generations.

However, the weak correlation between real wage improvement and marriage age decline suggests that other factors must have influenced the latter. Such factors may have been connected with employment patterns and the structure of the labour force. As the century wore on, farmers grew less inclined to have young farm workers living in the farmhouse, as had been usual in the past. One factor in this was an increase in arable farming, which needed a more seasonal workforce. Another was that some degree of population increase was already occurring, increasing labour supply and thus reducing the incentive to farmers to hoard labour by providing board and lodging. This encouraged independent living and, since two together can live more cheaply than two apart, marriage. Independence may also have reduced the moral and practical checks on sex before marriage and thus have led to an increase in premarital conception. Since religious beliefs were still strong, there was an incentive for the baby-in-waiting to be legitimised by marriage. By the later eighteenth century further changes in employment patterns provided stronger incentives still to early marriage. The growth of the labour force in rural areas in the south was not being matched by an increase in work opportunities and, in these circumstances, social pressures increasingly marginalised female employment in agriculture, especially in grain-growing areas. The ability of single women to support themselves was therefore reduced and, while marriage rarely led to prosperity, at least it guaranteed support from the husband's wage. Simultaneously, the ability of women and children to earn money from proto-industry increased. This was because until the 1780s or so the impact of powered machinery on textile manufacture was minimal. With output increasing, there was increased demand for hand-spinning and, although some regions had a much more developed textile industry than others, this demand reached into most parts of the kingdom. Even after cotton spinning began to be mechanised, weaving continued by hand and the demand for this continued to increase; during the Napoleonic Wars other cottage employments such as glove- and lace-making also prospered. In spite of women's employment, however, living standards in southern rural areas were falling from the late eighteenth century. As this occurred the Poor Law, which provided a mechanism for support of the poor, became more generously interpreted so that whole families, rather than just individual poor such as the elderly and orphans, received some financial help. Whilst historians used to think that this made no difference to birth rates, recent opinion is that it encouraged the pattern of early marriage and large families to continue.

There were, therefore, a number of reasons why marriage ages might have fallen which were unconnected with male wage rates. Other evidence supports the idea that these may not have been a major factor. In two market towns, Banbury and Gainsborough, there was little change in the age of marriage. Changes in real wages should have affected these settlements as they did others; but the type of occupation, the structure of the labour force and the availability and nature of women's work were less likely to have changed, at least up to the early nineteenth century.

Until quite recently most historical demographers thought that declining mortality had a greater impact on population change than rising fertility; they no longer think that, but the decline in mortality was still important. One factor was a decline in epidemics, not just in England but throughout Europe. There are various explanations for this, the most convincing of which is that, as trade grew and increasingly led to the mingling of populations, previously lethal diseases such as measles and smallpox spread and became relatively mild diseases of childhood, rather than killers that hit adult populations which had no inbuilt resistance. However, there may be other explanations for the reduction in epidemics including, quite simply, a decline in the virulence of certain key diseases. The other main component of the decline in mortality was a fall in infant mortality (the deaths of children under one year), from around 200 per thousand in the early eighteenth century to less than 150 per thousand in the early nineteenth century. Mortality caused by infection after birth hardly changed; the decline was almost entirely in endogenous mortality, that is mortality associated with the birth process itself, including prematurity. This can be directly associated with the decline in the number of stillbirths. It therefore seems likely that the same factor was at work: on current thinking this was a long-term improvement in nutrition which started in the early eighteenth century and whose beneficial effect continued for a time even after real wage levels had ceased to grow. By the early nineteenth century, however, the national average of mortality ceased to decline and remained static until it began to fall again from the 1860s. One likely reason for the long period of stagnation was a deterioration in mortality in large cities as they became dirtier and more crowded, counterbalancing a slight improvement elsewhere. Although fertility simultaneously fell, a wide gap had now opened up between the number of births and the number of deaths so from 1830 the population continued to increase, albeit more slowly than before.

Over the whole period, much of the population increase was independent of industrialisation. Agricultural improvement and the growth of trade lay behind the prosperity of the early and mid-eighteenth century. This encouraged earlier marriage and also improved maternal nutrition, thus in turn reducing stillbirths and endogenous infant mortality. In addition, there were declines in epidemic disease which were also independent of industrialisation. Later in the century the continuing propensity to marry young may have been influenced by changes in the structure of employment. These were only marginally influenced by industrialisation; they occurred in the deepest rural areas as well as elsewhere and were, in part, caused by the population growth that was already taking place. The growth of proto-industry was another factor, but this had been going on since the seventeenth century or earlier and was only weakly related to the growth of modern, powered industry. By the early nineteenth century the situation was different as wage rates had been pushed upwards in industrialising areas. So far as wages did influence the age of marriage – and their impact is uncertain – this may have helped people to continue to marry young in such areas. On the other hand, rural areas in the south were simultaneously experiencing growing poverty. Here it may have been the Poor Law which, by providing a safety net, helped to prevent the age of marriage from rising – another factor which was independent of industrialisation. From the 1820s onwards it becomes almost impossible to generalise about the causes of population increase. Uncontrolled urbanisation may have increased mortality, and industrialisation was associated with urbanisation although the two processes were not identical. In addition, the cheaper products of power-driven industry were now wrecking rural proto-industry and reducing the incentive that it gave to early marriage. However, changes in the Poor Law from 1834 which reduced its support for large families were nothing to do with industrialisation.

For the purposes of this chapter, the lack of much direct relationship between industrialisation and population growth up to the early nineteenth century is sufficient, because industrialisation was well under way by that time, and many of the big inventions had been made. Since population increase was an independent variable, the hypothesis that demand growth arising from this population increase was one cause of the Industrial Revolution remains a possibility, but a possibility is not a probability and the potential impact of such an increase on demand now needs to be examined.

The basic problem with the hypothesis that population increase fostered demand growth is that a growing population, without additions of land or capital or both, will experience diminishing returns. Each new recruit to the labour force will produce less until the next addition is zero or virtually zero and, as a result, incomes will not rise as fast as population. As the population continues to grow the addition to national income becomes ever smaller. So we need to see whether, notwithstanding the problem of decreasing returns, a rise in population could have increased the demand for goods and services to such an extent that it provided a significant impetus to industrialisation.

Joel Mokyr has calculated that the effects of population growth on demand would account for no more that 10 per cent or so of the actual rise in the output of industrial goods between 1750 and 1850. Mokyr's calculation is based on assumptions about decreasing returns. Land and capital are assumed to be static and technology unchanged. He assumes that the decline in income per person was constant throughout, which is unlikely – it would presumably be slower at the beginning when land and capital were still relatively abundant, and quicker later on. Therefore the figure of 10 per cent should be taken with a large pinch of salt, but nevertheless Mokyr's basic line of argument must be correct. With nothing but population growth, total national income would have grown but more slowly than population, so income per person would have fallen. Demand for more expensive goods and services would have actually declined. Only demand for food and the more basic industrial goods would have continued to increase.

However, there is another argument about population and demand: that, without the additional population, there would have been insufficient outlets for capital. The increase in population raised the return to capital, for instance in house-building and transport, and thus stimulated innovation and investment. This is the Keynesian argument as to why population increase might contribute to industrialisation, most famously put forward by the economist John Hicks. Instead of raising the demand for consumption goods, the rising population indirectly lifted the demand for capital goods; this increased total output and incomes, thus ensuring a further demand rise and so on. This would answer Mokyr's argument because, if population growth actually caused the investment rise, then the former was the prior cause of economic growth and arguments about decreasing returns are irrelevant.

In the first half of the eighteenth century investment rose without the benefit of population increase, as noted in Chapter 2. This does not prove that there was no connection between the two, but it is suggestive. Furthermore, on Mokyr's assumptions, population increase would not necessarily increase the demand for transport and housing. Declining incomes per person would force people to accept lower housing standards, while if demand for industrial goods grew only slowly there would be little incentive to improve transport. Mokyr's assumptions, if broadly accepted, also tell against the idea that invention, or investment in sectors with fast-changing technology, was stimulated by population growth. Declining incomes per person would retard increases in industrial production in these sectors too; and while innovation in textiles and iron will be discussed in Chapter 5, we can note that the great rush of invention in these industries came before the fastest and largest growth of population from 1780 onwards.

The relationship between population growth and land – meaning here simply agricultural land – is usually neglected in models of the Industrial Revolution, because it is assumed that land in Britain was always in short supply. Indeed, the problem of decreasing returns was originally seen as a problem related to the fixed supply of land. But if there was surplus land, population growth would only run into decreasing returns insofar as capital was short. And if it needed only quite small increments of capital for people to be set productively to work on new land, capital supply would not be a problem. So an assumption of flexible supplies of land may put population growth in a new light, and Mokyr's arguments about decreasing returns might need to be modified, particularly for the earlier part of this period.

There is evidence that there was more 'new land' – meaning land that was not used, or barely used, for productive purposes – in Britain than is often assumed. Agricultural enclosure took in commons and heaths which had previously been used for rough grazing, if they had been used at all. In many cases, especially in the north where population had been lower and agriculture more backward, these tracts of land were large. Arable, pasture and meadow land in England and Wales increased from 8.5 million hectares (21 million acres) in 1700 to over 12 million hectares (30 million acres) in 1850. The direct result of the additions was to increase agricultural rather than industrial output; but in acting to mitigate the decreasing returns from population growth, they meant that such growth might have a much more positive effect on aggregate incomes than was suggested earlier.

However, there were limits to what such new land could achieve. Most of it needed large, not small, amounts of capital to become productive. Enclosure was expensive because of the cost of fencing, draining and so on; opening up virgin heathland needed investment in new roads as well as in the land itself. Furthermore the land was often marginal agriculturally and so the increment to output, even after the application of capital, might not be large – although some new land, such as drained marshes, could be agriculturally rich. It is likely that the effect of adding new land has been underestimated and should be investigated more thoroughly, but it probably does not substantially change the sceptical view about the impact of population increase on demand.

Changes in taste

The idea that changing taste, or consumer preference, was one of the main motors behind a growth in demand for industrial goods is one of the more seductive explanations for the Industrial Revolution. In novels of the period, the flightier female characters eagerly discussed fashion, while newspapers and travel proliferated, spreading knowledge of new products rapidly over the country.

How might changing taste actually impact on industrial output? We must assume, first, that there was no prior rise in incomes: this has to be a prerequisite, as it has to be for all demand-side explanations of growth, since it is the rise in incomes that we are attempting to explain. Given that prerequisite, changes in taste might have acted to stimulate growth by calling forth extra effort as people strove to satisfy wants they had not previously had. Contemporary moralists tended to think that the poor, that is most of those who worked for wages, were liable to satisfy their immediate needs for food and shelter, and then spend the rest of the time in idleness. If this was true, its result in economic terms would be a backward-sloping supply curve for labour. Normally it is assumed that labour is a commodity like others. The higher the price the more labour is supplied, subject to the limits imposed by health and strength, as in the curve S1 in Figure 4.2. A backward-sloping curve embodies the assumption that people have a target income which is determined by their customary level of consumption. If wages rise, they reach their target income by doing less work and use the additional time in leisure. Beyond a certain level, therefore, higher wages call forth less work, as in the curve S2.

On the assumption that there was at some time in the past such a backward-sloping curve, then a reorientation of preferences towards consumption of goods rather than of leisure might be very important. It would increase aggregate incomes and therefore demand. It would also enhance labour supply and thus help the demand to be met, although that is a by-product of the hypothesis and not the central part of it.

There is evidence which seems to support this idea. In an ingenious piece of research, Hans-Joachim Voth reconstructed the working patterns of London workers by analysing the statements of witnesses at trials, to discover what they were doing at particular times and on particular days. He found that, between the middle and the end of the eighteenth century, there was a striking increase in hours worked: perhaps around one-third. This came about through workers ceasing to take off customary holy days and 'St. Monday' – the name given to Monday when it was added to Sunday to make a long weekend, as was often the case in mid-century.

This appears to show a growing taste for work by London workers, who were apparently prepared to work eleven-hour days, six days a week, since Saturday was a normal working day. However, there may be other explanations for the longer hours. E.P. Thompson saw them as a result of rigorous discipline by capitalists. This would not change the effect on demand although the motives for change would be different. A different picture emerges by focusing on London hourly wages which, in real terms, seem to have fallen substantially in the late eighteenth century – possibly by as much as 30 per cent. So by working far more hours, late eighteenth-century Londoners just about maintained their existing

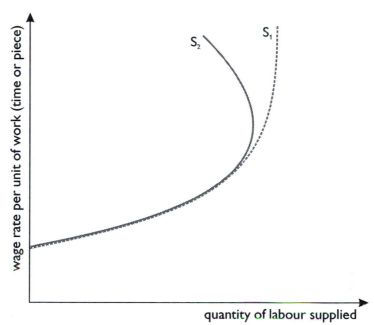

Figure 4.2 Backward-sloping labour supply curve

living standards. This neither proves nor disproves the backward-sloping supply curve; but neither does it suggest a growth in working-class demand, at least in London, since in spite of the extra hours worked Londoners were no better off.

Outside London, there is no comparable evidence, so one cannot say. It is likely that industrialists who had invested in expensive machinery did crack down on absenteeism as they wanted the machinery to be fully utilised; this was particularly the case when the machinery was powered by steam as the engine would run, and consume coal, whether there was much work being done or not. But the majority of workers, including most Londoners, still worked by hand and contemporary comment suggests that in the West Midlands, for instance, St. Monday was still taken. It may be that Voth's findings reflect a London phenomenon for which it is possible to find a London explanation. London hourly wages did not experience a special boost from industrialisation, while at the end of the century Londoners had to pay the high food prices characteristic of that war-torn period. Hence the fall in hourly real wage rates. On the other hand, because of the war there was usually plenty of demand for labour which, on this hypothesis, enabled Londoners to work harder to maintain their standard of living.

The verdict on the backward-sloping supply curve remains undecided. There may have been some shift towards a 'taste' for work – and income – as opposed to leisure. However, such a change was likely to have happened very slowly and was not complete by the early nineteenth century. For the poor, knowledge of and access to new goods were still limited. There were also physical constraints on consumerism: the small size of most workers' houses, combined with the need to bring up numerous children and to do paid work in domestic dwellings, must have put limits on the ability to acquire material goods. And in practice, whatever the shape of the supply curve for labour, it was unlikely to make much difference to the demand for industrial goods. This was because income levels for all the poor remained low, however hard they worked.

Evidence for this comes from Sarah Horrell's analysis of around 280 working-class budgets from the late eighteenth to the mid-nineteenth century. Over the period, real expenditure rose by about 30 per cent. (These are Horrell's figures; Feinstein's figures for real wages discussed in Chapter 7 would suggest a smaller gain.) Food absorbed by far the largest part of total spending, showing that a major priority was to diversify diet. Expenditure on rent increased and this may have represented some improvement in housing quality, although part of it was probably due to pressure on urban land. The shares of drink and tobacco, fuel, soap and candles, and clothing in total expenditure all remained roughly constant. This represented a modest increase in real terms for these items but again shows no dramatic change in tastes. The biggest relative increase in spending was on services – mainly education and sick-club subscriptions – but even by the mid-nineteenth century this was only about 2 per cent of the total. So working-class demand for industrial goods, apart from a few specific products, was minimal in the late eighteenth century, and was still very small in the mid-nineteenth.

Therefore, if changes in taste were a factor in raising demand for industrial goods, they must have operated via changes in demand from groups in the population other than workers. These groups would be the urban middle class, better-off farmers and the gentry. There is plenty of evidence that these groups were consuming more over time – indeed, they had to, because someone must have consumed the additional industrial goods which we know were produced. However, the question is not whether they consumed more but whether a change in their tastes, prior to a change in their incomes, initiated or contributed to large-scale industrialisation. If their increased consumption resulted from increasing incomes, then changes in taste would be more or less irrelevant.

Suppose their tastes had changed from one set of goods to another, for instance from pewter to china and other forms of pottery for tableware. The latter industries would have benefitted, but at the expense of pewter production. It may be that the industry which gained was able to reap economies of scale not available to that which lost, or had more potential for mechanisation, and so there would have been a beneficial chain reaction. But it would have happened on such a small scale in relation to the total economy that it could not have made a significant difference. A more intriguing notion is the possibility that taste changed, not from one consumer good to another, but from food to consumer goods. Since the diet of the middling to better off was quite good, it would have been feasible for expenditure to shift without their diet becoming inadequate, even if its variety declined. Numerous explanations have been put forward as to why changes in taste, of whatever kind, might occur. These explanations include emulation – the idea that the socially inferior copied the consumption patterns of their social superiors; and Colin Campbell's idea that there was an increasing propensity to consume, linked with the development of the romantic ethic. Campbell sees this as a set of ideas which developed in the eighteenth century and which gave a moral value to the experiencing of pleasure. Pleasure was gained from the sensation of novelty – as with a new purchase – and hence consumption became distanced from utility.

Lorna Weatherill's study of consumption between 1675 and 1725 provides evidence to test these explanations. Consumption of a range of household goods such as earthenware, clocks, prints, pictures and curtains was spreading rapidly at that time. This antedates Campbell's romantic ethic and suggests that, interesting though the idea is, it is not convincing. But emulation of social superiors does not fit the evidence either: many household goods were consumed first by middling social groups, not by the gentry. Obviously income and wealth were factors in consumption, but not the only ones. What seems to have been crucial to consumption patterns was access both to information and to the goods themselves. These things tended to go together, because information flowed with trade. So towns were more 'consumerist' than the countryside. But there were also regional differences: the northeast, for example, although fairly poor, had easy access to goods from London with which it had close links due to its coal shipments, so northeastern households had surprisingly high levels of consumer goods' ownership.

The most convincing explanation for such goods' increased consumption, therefore, is that it was based on knowledge and accessibility. These factors may have been reinforced by emulation, but of neighbours of similar social standing, not of the social elite; and they were probably also reinforced by the inherent desirability of the goods themselves. This does not mean that human beings have an inbuilt desire to own earthenware rather than pewter, or to put up curtains to shield themselves from public view; it merely means that most people desire some degree of novelty and adornment, whether of their household environment or their person. The new consumer goods of this period met these human needs; when people learned about such goods and could get hold of them they often wanted to buy them. This shift in consumption preferences is clearly indicative of a change in tastes, but could it have had so marked an effect on the demand for industrial goods as to stimulate industrialisation?

The first problem is uncertainty as to whether changing tastes acted largely to redistribute demand between different goods, rather than substantially increasing total demand for consumer goods. There is evidence that the price of many household goods was falling in the seventeenth and early eighteenth centuries, primarily because of greater efficiencies in manufacture and lower distribution costs. This being the case, some of the increase in consumption must have been due to these falling prices – a supply-side rather than a demand-side explanation. Taste would help to explain the different consumption decisions of individuals or small groups, and it is likely that changes in taste had some influence on everyone; but it would have played only a part in apportioning total demand between consumer goods and all other purchases, the other part being played by price changes.

The next problem is timing. After the 1720s Weatherill's sources, probate inventories, become rare and there is even less opportunity to tell whether changing tastes, or other factors, were at work. We do know that, with agricultural prices static or falling, in relative terms, until around 1750, the real incomes of middling groups were likely to be rising. So even if tastes ceased to change and remained static, these groups' demand for industrial goods was likely to have gone on rising, and such consumption evidence as there is bears this out. In practice, with better roads which stimulated information exchange and trade, the factors which kept tastes changing were still likely to be at work. However, just as the crucial period after 1750 got under way, agricultural prices started to rise relative to other prices. In the absence of supply-side improvements in industrial and trade productivity – which is exactly what we are trying to explain and so must be ruled out for the time being – the real income of middling groups would have fallen. Common sense, and most historians, rule out the possibility that agriculturalists were able to make up the shortfall in aggregate demand, once relative agricultural prices started to rise. Such rises only benefitted wealthier farmers and landowners; agricultural labourers, who had to buy food, were worse off, and poor farmers, who had to buy as much food as they sold, no better off. Wealthy farmers and landowners were an important segment of the population but there was no way that their gain, which in this simple model was entirely at the expense of other consumers, could have compensated for the decline in the latter's aggregate demand for industrial goods.

It seems very unlikely, therefore, that changing middle-class tastes could have single-handedly transformed the demand for consumer goods before and during industrialisation. So far as tastes did change, they did so in part because of the greater availability and increased knowledge of products. These developments in turn were partly due to improved transport and information networks and so 'taste', so far as it was important, cannot be seen as an abstract which changed in response to psychological changes among consumers; taste changed partly because of economic change elsewhere. It is also difficult to separate out changes in taste from the effects of price changes of goods themselves, or of boosts to consumer incomes resulting from falling food prices.

Even if tastes remained static, an increase in demand for consumer goods could have occurred because of a shift of income away from the poor and towards the middle classes, whose initial propensity to consume such goods was higher. But there is little evidence that there were long-term relative changes in money incomes. Chapter 7 suggests that middle-class consumers may have made real income gains because industrial goods and services declined in price relative to food. But such real income gains came about as a result of improvements in productivity and cannot be used to explain such improvements. As with changes in taste, therefore, changes in income distribution, so far as they occurred, were not likely to have led to significant increments in demand prior to or during the Industrial Revolution.

War

As the discussion in Chapter 1 indicated, there are two opposing interpretations of the effect of war on economic growth. In a Keynesian scenario, war could act to boost demand through increased government spending, which drew on unused savings and also enhanced incomes, thus allowing additional saving, which helped to finance government borrowing. In contrast, a neo-classical analysis sees war as absorbing scarce factors of production and therefore 'crowding out' investment: its effects on growth were deleterious. Of course, it is quite possible to believe that war had no significant effect one way or another on aggregate demand. However, even from this agnostic viewpoint one might accept that it could have had specific effects and these may have had some long-term impact: for instance, it might have boosted demand and led to economies of scale in some industries; alternatively, or as well, it might have had adverse economic effects through the disruption of trade.

The biggest criticism of the crowding-out thesis is that, during the Revolutionary and Napoleonic Wars (henceforth 'the wars'), which were by far the longest of the whole period, the investment ratio seems to have continued to rise. There was probably some shift of investment towards agriculture because of high food prices; but there is no evidence that industrial investment was significantly below the level it would have reached anyway. Given that the wars at their peak absorbed around 30 per cent of national income, this result is quite surprising. However, Chapter 2 showed that savings rose sharply to meet government demand for money. And the wars did not absorb labour needed for industrial production, because military recruits could be provided by rural labour-surplus areas such as the south of England, Scotland, Wales and Ireland. Unfortunately, there has been no intensive study of army recruitment patterns, but there seems to be some evidence to bear out this supposition. However, in spite of the endemic labour surplus in these areas, army demands and demands for increased agricultural production put a temporary strain on labour supply. There is evidence that because of this, female participation in waged work increased, having become marginalised in labour-surplus areas over the previous fifty years. In effect, the wars created work for the pool of Lewis-type surplus labour which, as Chapter 3 suggested, was not available to work in industry.

These two suppositions together, if true, would suggest a Keynesian interpretation of the wars' economic effects, in which capital and labour, previously in surplus, were now absorbed. The capital surplus is more problematic and, as Chapter 2 suggested, it is possible to find other explanations for the wartime increase in savings. The use in wartime of the rural labour surplus is likely, as suggested above; once the surplus was employed, it would generate extra tax revenue for the government through spending on dutiable goods such as beer, and thus reduce the amount which needed to be raised from savings. However, all this is a far cry from proving that the wars positively affected the long-term growth of the economy or even made it better off at the time. Innovation and a rising investment ratio were already well established. Furthermore the positive effects of the wars as set out above were likely to have been balanced by the negative. In particular, food prices were raised because of disruption of the European grain trade; this cut all consumers' incomes and, Glenn Hueckel has argued, capitalists' profits. The only people who definitely gained were landowners and wealthy farmers. And while Britain's naval supremacy enabled it to monopolise textile exports outside Europe, the foreign currency from this had to be spent to meet the rising prices of imports and the costs of the wars themselves.

War demand might have played a part in stimulating the growth of certain industries, particularly the metal industries. There were various possible mechanisms: higher profits could have led to higher investment; economies of scale could have reduced costs and, in the long term, prices; and learning-by-doing could have accelerated during war as output rose and, again, reduced costs in the long term. While all these could have occurred, the fact remains that the big inventions, in coke-smelting and puddling, had already been made before the wars began in 1792, and many of the civilian uses which were to transform the long-term demand for iron had also been pioneered earlier. These included iron rails, iron bridges and iron for building construction. Similar comments apply to other metal industries such as copper and lead, which had also been transformed in scale and scope well before the 1790s. In the medium term, the impact of the wars was probably delete-rious. They were followed by government fiscal retrenchment and an attempt to reverse wartime inflation by the restoration of ster-ling convertibility into gold, these measures causing a period of recession. At the same time, landowners and farmers refused to be weaned off high agricultural prices, which they hoped to perpet-uate through the notorious Corn Laws of 1815. By putting duties on foreign grain unless British prices rose particularly high, the Laws ensured that the wars were inimical to industrialisation long after the Battle of Waterloo had been fought and won.

Export growth

A neo-classical perspective on export-led growth is that resources would shift to those sectors, and away from others, in response to rising prices for the factors needed to produce the exports. This would produce some gains in income because economies of scale, if they were available in those sectors, would raise efficiency, and more certainly because there would be gains from trade. Britain would be more efficient at producing the goods it exported, foreign countries at producing the goods Britain imported, and so the income of both parties would rise. But the gains would take a long time to realise as resources shifted, while the positive effect on incomes would be limited as there would be losers – the industries making goods for which imports substituted – as well as gainers. In contrast, in a world of underemployed resources, export growth would have a more dynamic impact. Exports would draw on under-employed capital and labour, thus raising profits, investment and growth. However, the multiplier effect would be restricted as long as imports rose to match the growth in exports. If some or all of the increased exports were financed by British credit or by the import of bullion, thus raising the money supply, the multiplier effect would be evident as the additional spending would not all leak away in imports.

The potential contribution of exports to growth begs the question of what actually happened to them. The question centres upon the proportion of exports in total industrial output, the timing of export growth, and the issue of whether such growth was dependent upon, or independent of, prior import growth.

There are still uncertainties in our knowledge of the proportion of industrial growth accounted for by exports. These exist because of gaps in the statistics and also because of the extreme difficulty of developing reliable price series over long periods. However, Javier Cuenca Esteban has recently suggested that the role of exports may have been underestimated in the past. Industrial exports may have grown almost eightfold, in constant price terms, over the eighteenth century and tripled again between 1801 and 1831. If true this is impressive, as is Cuenca Esteban's calculation that exports could have contributed 50–80 per cent of the growth of industrial production between 1780 – admittedly a depressed year because of the American war – and 1801. He also finds that 1760–80, hitherto written off as a period of low export growth, scores better. Finally, export growth was clearly important in the pre-1760 period but not as important as later. This suggested trajectory of growth ties in quite well with the generally accepted notion that domestic demand for industrial goods was buoyant in the first half of the eighteenth century, when low food prices were combined with moderate population growth (see Table 4.2).

Exports may have grown rapidly, particularly in the later eighteenth century, but that does not automatically mean that they were exogenous to industrial growth. Increasing exports may have been a response rather than a cause. For instance, it has been suggested that imports led exports. In other words, rising domestic demand sucked in imports, which then gave foreign purchasers the wherewithal to buy British exports. Econometric testing suggests that this was not the case, however, and that periods of export growth preceded periods of import growth. However, export growth may have been caused, not by rising overseas demand, but by earlier falls in the prices of British manufactures relative to the price of imports. In economic terminology, the demand schedule of the overseas buyers remained the same, but like all buyers, they purchased more if price fell relative to their income. The alternative is that foreign demand genuinely rose, or in economic terms, the demand curve shifted to the right. There is a simple if crude method of testing this by examining the terms of trade. This is a ratio, obtained by dividing the index of export prices by the index of import prices. If the former fell whilst the latter stayed the same, then the terms of trade are said to have moved against the exporting country, and vice versa. A deterioration in Britain's terms of trade, that is a fall in the relative prices of British exports, would imply that a growth in export volumes was partly a response to this price fall. But if the terms of trade remained stable, then the goods which Britain imported must have been changing in price at the same rate as British exports, and there would have been no spur to British exports from a fall in their relative price. This holds with even more force if the terms of trade were moving in Britain's favour. In reality, Britain's terms of trade, while deteriorating somewhat in the first half of the eighteenth century, improved again in the second half when the rise in exports was most dramatic. This suggests that demand curves in importing countries were shifting to the right; in other words, foreign demand was rising and export growth was, at least in part, exogenous to industrial growth.

The pattern of export growth also fits in with this picture. Over the eighteenth century, exports to Europe rose absolutely, but declined sharply as a proportion of the total: from 85 per cent in 1700–01 to 49 per cent in 1772–3, and then under the impact of war to only 30 per cent in 1797–8. By contrast, export to the Americas – the North American colonies, the West Indies and South America – rose from 10 per cent to 37 per cent to 57 per cent of the total at the same dates. Exports to the rest of the world – mainly Africa and India – made up the total. In the case of Europe, there were modest rises in income in the early eighteenth century which would have increased demand. From mid-century, however, Europe like Britain was experiencing population increase which put pressure on land and food supplies. Unlike Britain, Europe was

experiencing only limited industrial growth to take up the population surplus, and therefore European living standards tended to
decline. As a result, demand for British exports was unlikely to have
been buoyant after mid-century, and this is reflected in the export
figures. But American demand was expanding rapidly, and it was
expanding for reasons which were rooted in the Americas. The
population of the thirteen North American colonies which
declared independence in 1776 and became the United States
expanded from 250,000 in 1700 to over two million in 1770.
Britain made some contribution to this in the form of emigration;
but as the natural rate of population increase was very high, three-
quarters or more of the growth was American-made. Crucially,
America had land.

Georg Borgstrom has coined the striking phrase 'ghost acreage'
for such land – land that was always there, but only became assimi-
lated to the European world as it was settled or as the native Americans were dispossessed. This ghost acreage permitted European
settlers to escape decreasing returns and instead work productively.
Relatively little British capital was needed, because the settlers' own
labour constructed many of the capital assets that were needed,
such as buildings and roads. As the Americans' prosperity grew,
their ability to accumulate their own capital increased. With almost
unlimited land, American standards of living were high once capital
assets had been constructed, and so they could afford to purchase
British manufactures.

There was one major exception to this, and that was the income
created by slavery. The profits of the slave trade itself contributed
only a small part of this income. The bulk of it came from the
labour of the slaves themselves, which was transmitted into products – at first mainly sugar, then towards the end of the eighteenth
century North American cotton. The sale of these products transmitted itself into demand for British goods, including clothes and
implements for the slaves. So in contrast to eighteenth-century
North America, the West Indian market was largely created by
demand from Europe for colonial goods, although the availability
of fertile land was as necessary for economical supply as were slaves
and British capital to establish the plantations.

In spite of these caveats, export growth was likely to have had an
exogenous demand-side influence on growth in the wider economy.
As suggested earlier in this section, on the assumption of surplus

capital and labour, substantial growth possibilities might flow from the autonomous growth of export demand; on neo-classical assumptions some, but more limited, possibilities. Whether or not there was surplus capital for investment is problematic, while if there was originally a labour surplus in industrialising regions, much of it was soon absorbed. Such small amounts of capital were needed for machinery, however, that the question of surplus is virtually irrelevant, as only a small division of existing resources would have been needed to provide enough productive capital to meet the additional export demand. And the diminution of the labour surplus does not tell against the export-led growth model as much as it does against Lewis, for whom an increase in investment was dependent on surplus labour. A view of the Industrial Revolution, based on the assumption that there was an emerging labour surplus in the mid-eighteenth century, could encompass a once-and-for-all boost to economic growth from an export boom starting in that period which absorbed slack in the economy. This was self-sustaining, as savings rose to match further demands for investment stemming from the increase in invention. The labour surplus might diminish, but population growth would ensure a steady flow of labour to match the increase in demand.

However, this does not in itself explain invention and innovation, and it remains to be seen whether demand-side changes can be linked with these phenomena.

Tables

Table 4.1 Population in Britain 1751–1851

	Total (millions)	Average decadal rate of growth	
1751	7.5	1751–1801	7%
1801	10.5	1801–1851	15%
1851	20.8		

After R. Woods, The Population of Britain in the Nineteenth Century (1992)

Table 4.2 Exports

	I	II
1700	100	22%
1760	222	31%
1780	355	28%
1801	793	39%
1831	2,312	18%

After J.C. Esteban, 'British industrial exports', Table 1 (see further reading)

I   Index of exports at constant prices. This serves as a volume measure, not of total tonnage, but rather of the increase in exports of different types of goods when their prices are held constant at 1800 levels. From 1780 the figures are the result of averaging volumes over 11 years

II Exports' share of gross industrial output at current prices; the fall between 1801 and 1831, in spite of the rapid volume increase, is due to the fall in the price of textile exports

Further reading

J. Mokyr, 'Demand versus supply in the industrial revolution' in J. Mokyr *The Economics of the Industrial Revolution* (1985) deals succinctly with the role of demand factors from a neo-classical standpoint, not surprisingly finding that they cannot sustain explanatory weight. B. Fine and E. Leopold, *The World of Consumption* (1993) echoes this and is perhaps more readable; it is also valuable for changes in taste. R.S. Schofield, 'British population change 1700–1871' in R. Floud and D. McCloskey, *The Economic History of Britain* (see Introduction) is the best summary of the likely reasons for population change. J.R. Hicks' famous comment about the effect of population increase is in *Value and Capital* (2nd ed., 1946), p. 302: 'perhaps the whole Industrial Revolution of the last two hundred years has been nothing but a vast secular boom, largely induced by the unparalleled rise in population'. L. Weatherill, *Consumer Behaviour and Material Culture in Britain 1660–1760* (1996) is an outstanding survey of consumer behaviour. J. Brewer and R. Porter, *Consumption and the World of Goods* (1993) has a host of valuable chapters. For working-class consumption see S. Horrell, 'Home demand and British industrialisation', *JEH*, 56 (1996), pp. 561–604. P.K. O'Brien and S.L. Engerman, 'Exports and the growth of the British economy from the Glorious Revolution to the Peace of Amiens', in B. Solow, *Slavery and the Rise of the Atlantic System* (Cambridge, 1991) is the best short survey of exports. The reference to ghost acreage comes from E.L. Jones, *The European Miracle* (Cambridge, 1981).

R. Burt, 'The transformation of the non-ferrous metals industries in the 17th and 18th centuries', *EcHR*, 48 (1995), pp. 23–45.

C. Campbell, *The Romantic Ethic and the Spirit of Modern Consumerism* (Oxford, 1987); also 'Understanding traditional and modern patterns of consumption in eighteenth-century England: a character-action approach' in Brewer and Porter, *Consumption*.

R. Davis, *The Industrial Revolution and British Overseas Trade* (Leicester, 1979).

J.C. Esteban, 'The rising share of British industrial exports in industrial output, 1700–1851', *JEH*, 57 (1997), pp. 879–906.

T.J. Hatton, J.S. Lyons and S.E. Satchell, 'Eighteenth-century British trade: homespun or empire made?' *Explorations in Economic History*, 20 (1983), pp. 163–82.

G. Hueckel, 'War and the British economy, 1793–1815: a general equilibrium analysis', *Explorations in Economic History*, 10 (1973), pp. 365–96.

P.K. O'Brien, 'European economic development' (see Chapter 2).

D.A. Reid, 'The decline of St. Monday 1776–1876', *Past and Present*, 71 (1976), pp. 78–101.

C. Shammas, 'Change in English and Anglo-American consumption from 1550–1800' in Brewer and Porter, *Consumption*.

S.D. Smith, 'The market for manufactures in the thirteen continental colonies 1698–1776', *EcHR*, 51 (1998), pp. 676–708.

E.P. Thompson, 'Time, work-discipline and industrial capitalism', *Past and Present*, 38 (1967), pp. 56–97.

H.J. Voth, 'Time and work in eighteenth-century London', *JEH*, 58 (1998), pp. 29–58.

E.A. Wrigley, 'Explaining the rise in marital fertility in England in the "long" eighteenth century', *EcHR*, 51 (1998), pp. 435–64.

E.A. Wrigley and R.S. Schofield, *The Population History of England 1541–1871* (Cambridge, 1981).

E.A. Wrigley, R.S. Davies, J.E. Oeppen and R.S. Schofield, *English Population History from Family Reconstitution 1580–1937* (Cambridge, 1997) (see Chapters 8 and 9 for modifications to the findings in *The Population History of England*).

Chapter 5

Inventors and entrepreneurs

While the majority of accounts of the Industrial Revolution agree that invention and innovation were crucial in one way or another, the possible reasons for invention are a subject of hot debate. Exogenous growth theory sees invention as occurring outside the economic system. Scientific advance, amateur tinkering or sheer random discovery may all be factors. There are different versions of endogenous growth theory. A composite of the main lines of approach would start with profit-seeking as the motivation for invention. Profit-seeking in turn is encouraged by the opportunity to gain favourable market positions. The size of the market and the cost of invention are important components in the likely rate of profit. This emphasis on invention, and subsequent innovation, through profit-seeking is sometimes called neo-Schumpeterian. Once the process of invention has begun it might be accelerated in various ways. Earlier inventions, by making new processes possible, open up new opportunities for learning-by-doing, perhaps in turn leading to a series of microinventions or even a new macroinvention. Human capital is important in endogenous growth theory: inventors themselves possess human capital while, in addition, a good and relatively cheap supply of skilled labour facilitates research and development, because the construction of prototype machines needs more skilled labour than does mass-producing existing varieties.

The neo-Schumpeterian emphasis on profit-seeking, while it has an obvious similarity with Schumpeter's own position, is not identical with it. From a neo-classical perspective, as innovation promotes profit opportunities (using profit in the Schumpeterian sense of higher than normal returns), all businessmen are potentially likely to innovate since businessmen, by definition, seek profits. Of course, lack of capital and constraints on entering unfamiliar lines of business prevent many businessmen from adopting specific changes, but in principle it is usual and normal for businessmen to innovate. Both exogenous and endogenous growth theories, therefore, tend to lay the emphasis on the importance of the original invention, rather than on subsequent innovation, on the grounds that entrepreneurial behaviour is the norm rather than the exception. Schumpeter's insistence on the scarcity of entrepreneurs is not often taken up in modern theoretical approaches, although, as we shall see, it finds an echo among some historians.

These theoretical standpoints generate a set of questions about the Industrial Revolution. First, did invention increase? If so, what were its sources? In particular, were they partly or largely outside the economic system? Or were they inside it, a consequence of human capital formation, of learning-by-doing, or of an active search for profits? Second, was innovation by businessmen a relatively normal aspect of economic activity, or did it need a rare and special breed of entrepreneurs? If the latter were vital, then we ought to seek out factors in society which developed entrepreneurship. It may be that all these theories have something to tell us. It is perfectly logical, for instance, to suggest that a process of exogenous invention sparked off rapid change but that this was carried forward endogenously; and that all businessmen sought profit, but often imperfectly, and, as a result, the entrepreneur's special foresight – the quality on which Schumpeter laid most emphasis – was still important.

Inventors

Measuring invention is very difficult. The only hard and fast figures are for patents, which allowed sole exploitation of an invention for fourteen years, a period which was sometimes extended. Patents were originally one of many types of royal grant, and as such came to be viewed by the government largely as a money-making device. As a result, they were expensive to obtain, making patent statistics not exactly what they seem. The cost of a patent averaged around £120, a respectable middle-class income for a year in the mid-eighteenth century; added to this were the two months or so a patentee had to spend in London in order to circumnavigate the bureaucracy. When all this was taken into account, in many industries patenting did not seem worth the trouble. In process industries such as brewing, so much depended on knack and skill that patents did not give much extra protection. Inventions in other industries were often protected by secrecy, inventors going to considerable lengths to guard special machinery and prevent most of their workers from using it. By contrast, in some industries, such as textiles up to the late eighteenth century, the diffused nature of an occupation carried on in houses and workshops up and down the country made attempts to prevent the illegal use of a patent very difficult, with the result that many small inventions in this industry went unpatented. From the mid-eighteenth century on, however, the patent system became more accessible. As incomes rose, the real cost of patents fell, while transport improvements made it easier to travel to London to secure a patent. These factors helped to accelerate the rate of patenting. Christine MacLeod argues that the increased propensity to patent then developed its own momentum: inventors became anxious to protect themselves and therefore struck first by registering a patent, rather than simply assuming that no one else would think of their idea.

A great deal of invention never found its way into the patent statistics but, as time went by, it is likely that a higher proportion of inventions were patented. As a result, the rise in patents, from an average of nine per annum in the 1750s to twenty-nine per annum in the 1770s and sixty-five per annum in the 1790s, is not a reliable guide to the amount of inventive activity, although unfortunately, rather sweeping hypotheses have been constructed on the basis of this increase. Finally, it is worth remembering that some of the most important new ideas, especially those in service industries or involving organisation, were unpatentable. Among these were canals, turnpikes, financial techniques such as mortgages and bills, and the concept of factories.

In spite of all these caveats, most historians would agree that part of the growth in the number of patents reflected a genuine increase in invention, although it is difficult to say how great that was. And many of the inventions which all agree were outstandingly important came in the second half of the eighteenth century, notably the three types of spinning machine: the jenny (1760s), roller-spinning (later known as the water frame, 1760s–70s although based on ideas going back to the 1730s) and the mule (1770s). Equally important were the powerloom (1790s), iron puddling (1780s) and Watt's improvements to the steam engine (1760s–80s). Exogenous growth theory suggests that this happened for reasons outside the existing economic and technical framework. However, it is difficult to find examples in which this was clearly the case. Science, usually regarded as exogenous, helped in some chemical innovations and, through instruments such as the thermometer, in other process industries. The ideas behind the first steam engines in the early eighteenth century were discussed by a number of eminent scientists. But James Watt, although a scientific instrument maker and well versed in science, owed little to theory and evolved his improvements through practical inventiveness. The vast bulk of eighteenth-century inventions, including all the famous textile machines and the innovations in iron-making, were made by practical men or inventive amateurs and not by scientists. Of these two groups, the inventive amateur was less important. Edmund Cartwright, the originator of the powerloom and the wool-combing machine, was the most obvious amateur – a clergyman who only started his inventive career when he was forty-one. But Cartwright relied on skilled workmen to construct his experimental machines; and while he spent a fortune on his experiments, he hoped for a substantial payoff, although it never materialised. So his inventive activity was not purely amateur but relied on professional assistance and had some pecuniary motive. Watt and many other practical inventors shared with Cartwright a strong technical curiosity, but in most cases this had to be accompanied by a realistic appraisal of the economics of their projects, because otherwise they would never have got off the ground; few inventors could afford Cartwright's cavalier approach to money.

Although exogenous growth theory does not get much support from the evidence, some still see a place for it. The most important voice has been that of Nick Crafts, who stresses the randomness in inventive activity. In an influential article published in 1977 he argued that both Britain and France had dynamic textile industries in the mid-eighteenth century. In both countries there was active experimentation to improve techniques, so it was likely that the inventions in spinning would have been hit on sooner or later, but chance that they were discovered in Britain rather than France. Given the importance of learning-by-doing, the initial location of the inventions facilitated a rapid spread and improvement of the machines in Britain. France was not immediately able to make up the early slippage and then, from the Revolution on, suffered twenty-five years of disruption, by which time British technology had consolidated its lead.

Crafts' argument applies chiefly to the textile industry. However, Crafts sees this industry's early and rapid growth as radically skewing the direction industrialisation took in Britain, and hence the importance he places on it. Certainly the argument cannot be confidently applied to the coal, iron and other metal industries. As Chapter 3 suggested, human capital was important in these industries and was developed through the accumulation of skills, which had been built up through generations of working and using coal. This human capital was beneficial to the process of invention and innovation as many new processes involved years, sometimes decades, of trial and error in which inventors and skilled workers together could sort out problems. Thus the smelting of iron with coke rather than charcoal was first undertaken by Abraham Darby I in 1709, but did not take off until the 1750s. It seems likely that the accumulation of knowledge over this period led to reduced coke consumption until a cross-over point was reached at which coke-smelted pig-iron became decisively cheaper than charcoal-smelted iron. (Pig was iron in its crude state, for subsequent casting or for conversion to wrought iron, which was used instead of steel – then very expensive – when tensile strength was required.) Various factors were involved in this development, but learning-by-doing was an important part of it. The inventive process antedated 1709, as the use of coal and coke in copper-smelting, something with which Darby was familiar, had been developed from the 1680s. Similarly, the use of coke for converting pig to wrought iron was developed and improved from the 1760s on, first through the potting process and then in Henry Cort's puddling process. The potting process was a dead-end but it was widely used for a short period and illustrates that inventive activity in the industry was widespread. The puddling process depended on the reverberatory furnace, which was the technique used in copper-smelting from the 1680s, thus bringing us full circle. These connections illustrate how coal-using techniques could ramify throughout the metal industries, but also how these techniques usually developed slowly because they required much practice to perfect.

Central to Crafts' argument is the textile industry itself. While it is true that the French textile industry was large, Crafts perhaps overstresses its ability to develop inventions to a workable state even supposing that they had been made in France first. Macroinventions in textiles, as in iron, required a period of development in which skilled mechanics helped to perfect them. Once in a workable state, a good supply of skilled workmen meant that the machines could be built cheaply. Finally, skilled workmen would usually make further small improvements, or microinventions, to the machine. Britain almost certainly had an advantage over France in the supply of skilled mechanics, at first working mainly in wood but increasingly in iron. Iron was a far better material for constructing machinery, being both lighter in proportion to its strength, and harder and therefore better for gear wheels and other components. It is difficult to see how France could easily have maintained a lead over Britain even if it had initially gained one through making the inventions first, since French understanding of the capability of metals for machinery construction was much less developed.

Even when there was a workable invention, the French seem to have had problems in incorporating it into production – that is, in innovation. An example was the flying, or fly, shuttle for weaving, devised by John Kay in the 1730s. For technical reasons this was slow to penetrate the weaving of woollens in England, but made rapid progress in cotton-weaving. Kay was dissatisfied with his treatment in England and in 1747 went to France, where the government supported him in the dissemination of this and other improvements. But in spite of that support, the shuttle made slower progress in France than in England.

It seems likely that the absence of a depth of technical expertise – human capital – and hence the slowness of learning-by-doing was a major factor in the slow rate of innovation in the French textile industry. Poor communications may also have been a consideration. But whether the initial inventions were quite as random as Crafts has suggested is a moot point. It seems oddly coincidental that all the major successful inventions in textiles – the flying shuttle and other improvements to weaving, the spinning machines, and the carding machine which was perfected by Arkwright in 1775 but had been in use earlier – were actually made in Britain. Harry Dutton's important book on invention, published in 1984, emphasised the value of the patent system, in spite of its defects and expense, in encouraging invention: aspiring inventors responded to the opportunity it gave to reap superprofits; they were 'economic men operating in .... an invention industry'. In other words, they conceived of their job as inventing, their profit coming from patenting inventions and selling the rights to use them, as opposed to making their inventions within a trade in which they had always worked.

Dutton's insight is very important but his criterion for such 'economic men' – that they spent all their time inventing – should not be taken too literally: an 'invention industry', in the sense of a substantial group of full-time inventors, did not exist in the mid-eighteenth century and only became important later as the patent system became more accessible and cheaper. However, it is still true that from an early date most inventors were actuated by economic motives; they saw invention as a way of making money although they were not necessarily in a position to spend all their time on it. Lewis Paul and John Wyatt, for instance, developed the idea of roller-spinning in 1738, although they never succeeded in making it economic; they had made other inventions, both in the textile and clothing industry and outside it, but like most eighteenth-century inventors they tended to use their inventions themselves rather than, or as well as, selling off the rights. Whether they exploited their own invention or not, for most inventors the idea that they were making an investment which would yield a profit seems to have been there in one way or another. Thus Watt wrote in 1785: 'In consequence of the security which we imagined these exclusive [patent] privileges gave, we have for many years devoted our time and money to the bringing the invention to perfection ... yet we have not hitherto acquired such sums of money by it as should make it be esteemed an enviable concern were the profits to terminate at this juncture'.

Once a process of invention and innovation was under way in particular industries, other factors became important. Firms specialising in the production of capital goods – textile machinery and steam engines early on, and by the early nineteenth century machine tools and paper-making machinery – emerged. Once patents on the early macroinventions had expired, these firms exploited them, differentiating their product by constant microinventions. This further accelerated the rate of patenting and can give a misleading picture of the growth of inventiveness, since previously such small improvements had often gone unpatented. Nevertheless there was a real increase in the impetus to invention: previously it had either been random or depended on a few highly motivated individuals; now there were firms whose success depended on it.

Another popular explanation of inventive activity can be seen as a variation of endogenous growth theory. This is the 'challenge and response' model, which suggests that a macroinvention sets up demand pressures within an industry, which encourage further inventions. One frequently cited instance is the textile industry, in which the increased productivity of weaving as a result of Kay's and other improvements gave inventors an incentive to improve spinning. However, the causal mechanism of such links is never carefully specified. In this case, the implication is that the increase in demand for cotton yarn for cloth drove up spinners' wages; but to show that such an increase was a result of the improvements in weaving would require a study of the textile industry in order to demonstrate that increased cloth production was caused, to a significant extent, by a fall in the price of cloth caused by these improvements. Other factors, such as better organisation, could have reduced costs and therefore prices in the industry; or wholly extraneous demand growth might have led to increased production. In practice all these factors were probably at work, but irrespective of these the potential productivity increase from mechanising spinning was so enormous that the wages of spinners were really a secondary consideration. Because of this, the idea of spinning machines goes back to the seventeenth century. The lack of success of such machines until the 1760s was not because the economic motive only appeared at that time, but because such machinery posed difficult technical problems and was very expensive to develop, as Paul and Wyatt found.

A slightly different argument has been developed to explain the adoption of coke-smelting in the iron industry, in which the rising price of charcoal has been seen as the challenge. In this case, the cause of the price rise was not a prior invention but simply the increasing demand for wood, for iron production and other purposes. While this encouraged the diffusion of coke-smelting, a lengthy period of experimentation had been necessary first, leading to increased fuel efficiency which was complemented by falling coke prices. Thus the mid-century rise in the price of charcoal was only one side of the cost equation and was not relevant to the original adoption of the technique by Abraham Darby. In the course of time, coke-smelting was likely to have overtaken charcoal-smelting anyway, unless wood was extremely cheap as it was in North America; the rise in charcoal prices merely accelerated this by a few years.

Both the models above are based on the idea that changes in the relative price of factors might stimulate invention. Presumably, a similar idea lies behind demand-side accounts of invention, which seem to assume that price changes, sparked off by demand changes, provided the incentive to invent. In Chapter 4 we saw that only one element of demand – exports – was likely to have grown rapidly enough to have had even the potential to provide such an incentive. Thus the jump in real wages in the north of England from around 1770 could be explained as a consequence of growing North American demand for textiles. However, the neo-classical objection to demand changes remains: if other prices rose simultaneously, then the incentive to invention would not have increased, since profit margins would have remained the same. As noted earlier, it is more likely that the spinning inventions were the fruition of a search process which had gone on for a considerable period. The assumption of a Keynesian-type economy in which capital and labour were in surplus is no more help, because if that was the case their price would not rise in spite of rising demand. Profits and capital accumulation would increase but there would be no spur to the rate of invention, thus providing a succinct refutation of any direct connection between demand-led growth and invention. An indirect stimulus from faster output growth, for instance by the acceleration of learning-by-doing, might remain.

There is a possible exception when a rapid shift in the demand for goods raises the demand for one factor of production whose supply is inelastic: there will be a temporary jump in the price of that factor and, if other factors' prices do not change, a possible spur to invention. A concrete example is the early surge in the demand for cottons for the West African trade in the late 1730s. This trade depended on imported yarn of a particular quality, and for various reasons imports had temporarily dried up. This induced a merchant in the trade, James Johnson, to buy licences to use the Paul and Wyatt machine, which still needed much development. Demand was therefore a factor in facilitating the improvement of the machine (not that it was ever perfected); but it did not play a part in its original conception, while development money also came from a number of sources apart from the cloth trade. This partial example of a direct relationship between the price of a factor – or in this case its complete non-availability – and invention seems very rare in the case of macroinventions. With microinventions, the cost of the invention and the time it takes to develop may be much less, and therefore the response to temporary changes in factor prices can be made quickly. Even here, however, the evidence suggests that learning-by-doing and human capital play a more important part in the process of invention. The search to reduce the fuel consumption of steam engines, for instance, was constant since fuel was an expensive item whatever the temporary fluctuations in its price.

So there is neither a very convincing theory nor much hard evidence to link either changes in factor prices, or more general shifts in demand, with invention. There is, however, both theory and evidence to link invention with market size. Alwyn Young and others have pointed out that larger markets provide larger profit incentives to reward inventors. Since the cost of developing inventions to a workable state was considerable, this is intuitively plausible for the Industrial Revolution period. Thus Arkwright claimed to have spent £13,000 by 1774, and Boulton and Watt almost certainly spent more. Accounts differ as to the cost of the Fourdrinier continuous paper-making machine (a French invention which was almost wholly developed in Britain) but at least £8,000 was spent in Britain from 1802 to 1807, exclusive of the costs of the original invention. The potentially higher rewards from a larger market would be relevant both to Dutton's lone inventors, and MacLeod's profit-seeking machinery firms which patented in order to secure a competitive advantage. Once inventions began to diffuse, there were private returns to the inventor – the licence fee to operate the patent and so forth – and also public benefits, which could be called knowledge spillovers.

One way of conceptualising knowledge spillovers is to see knowledge itself as a factor of production which has special qualities. 'Knowledge capital' can, unlike labour or physical capital, be applied again and again, if it is appropriate to a particular technology. This could happen even while a patent was in force, since the patentee might not be able to specify the patent in a way which covered all the knowledge embodied in it, and would certainly happen once the patent lapsed. Gillian Cookson has shown how, in the early nineteenth-century Yorkshire engineering industry, there was constant interaction between employers and skilled workers through training and subcontracting. These links can be modelled as the provision of frequent opportunities for knowledge spillovers, from both patented and non-patented inventions.

The existence and use of knowledge capital are related to market size in three ways: first, it is produced more rapidly if invention and innovation are more rapid, which they are likely to be with a larger market; second, the denser the network of production the more opportunity for knowledge spillovers as indicated above; third, the larger the economy the more likely it is that knowledge capital from one industrial sector will be of use in another. Thus the steam engine in Britain was successively used for pumping, increasing the blast in blast furnaces, driving stationary machinery, then steam-ships and then railway locomotives. More generally, techniques for machine-making including the use of machine tools could spill across a wide range of sectors.

A substantial market size is therefore the last ingredient needed for an endogenous growth model of the Industrial Revolution. The British market for industrial products was large by the mid-eigh-teenth century and continued to grow. Demand for consumer goods – particularly textiles, but also earthenware, iron kitchen utensils, and so on – was already high in the early part of the century and went on rising. This resulted in a large and growing market for machinery to produce such goods. From the later part of the century this expanded the market for steam engines which helped to drive machinery. More coal was needed, to power machinery and produce iron, and this necessitated more steam engines to pump water from mines. In the first half of the century the market grew largely because of domestic factors, and in the second half export growth became important. One reason for the original market growth was invention, which reduced costs and thus raised real incomes, as well as offering new products. An argument which relates invention positively to market size may therefore seem circular, but is not, because invention was only one of several causal factors in the original enlargement of the market. So it is logical to suggest that, as the market size grew, it encouraged inventions, which in turn further increased market size, and so on in a virtuous circle. Estimating the possible impact of increased market size on returns to invention would be an almost impossible task, since the estimate would need to take into account the decline in the relative cost of invention. And market size would only affect the returns to some inventions, primarily those which were made to be sold or licensed to others; inventions which were kept secret would usually have only a small market. Nevertheless all the macroinventions listed earlier were patented, and important eighteenth-century inventors such as Arkwright, and Boulton and Watt, saw licence fees as a major source of income.

The combination of market size and the patent system encouraged a search process for inventions. Once inventions were made a number of factors, notably human capital endowment and its further development, and knowledge spillovers, facilitated the development and improvement of these inventions. Crafts' basic point, that the search process which generated inventions could not have been guaranteed to produce successful ones only in Britain, is logically correct. But the initial odds that such inventions would be made in Britain – as actually happened – were almost certainly much higher than he seems to allow. And the likelihood that, wherever inventions were made, Britain would have been quicker and more effective at adopting them – as also happened – was very high indeed.

Market size is also relevant to innovation, and its potential significance to this is such that it will be treated separately in the next chapter. Innovation is the work of the entrepreneur, thus bringing us to this figure, whom Schumpeter saw as so central to dynamic economic change.

Entrepreneurs

Inventors and entrepreneurs were frequently the same persons, although to maintain clarity we should see the two as separate functions. Arkwright and Cort, for instance, were inventors, and entrepreneurs who used their inventions in various ways to make money, in Cort's case not very successfully. To Schumpeter such entrepreneurs were heroes who, like all heroes, were in short supply. The heroic entrepreneur has been seen by others apart from Schumpeter as a central figure of the Industrial Revolution.

Historians who focus on the psychology of the individual are naturally attracted to explanations which put individuals, rather than impersonal economic forces, at the forefront. Such explanations have never really recovered from their early association with primitive Freudianism, in which the alleged obsession by the middle-class family with potty-training encouraged in infants a love of money and thus led to the growth of capitalism; or as an early psychoanalyst put it, 'The sense of value attaching to money is a direct continuation of the sense of value that the infant attaches to its excretory product'.

In truth, there was nothing new about the love of money. Pre-industrial monarchs and landowners loved money; it was just that they obtained it in different ways from entrepreneurs. Max Weber, the German sociologist, in his 1904 book *The Protestant ethic and the spirit of capitalism*, argued that Protestantism encouraged asceticism and a rational attitude to the world and thus fostered capitalism. Since eighteenth-century Britain had already been Protestant for two hundred years, this much-criticised thesis is hardly relevant to our subject. The suggestion has been made that it was dissenting Protestants – Baptists, Quakers, Unitarians and later in the period Methodists – who were likely to become successful businessmen. But dissenters comprised only 15 per cent of the very wealthy with non-landed fortunes born between 1720 and 1860. While this is more than the proportion of dissenters in the population, it certainly does not prove a Weberian-type argument: if 85 per cent of the very wealthy were not dissenters, it would be absurd to suggest that economic growth depended on those who were. Even for this group, it has been suggested that the high degree of trust which existed in small religious groupings, leading to cheap and reliable access to credit, was more important than religious doctrine or upbringing.

So both evidence and common sense suggest that there were no special circumstances in the eighteenth century to produce an upsurge in the number of heroic entrepreneurs, exhibiting Schumpeterian qualities of drive and foresight. Nor do the entrepreneurs themselves necessarily fit this model. Edward Pease and George Philips were mentioned in Chapter 2; Pease founded the Stockton and Darlington railway and comes close to the Schumpeterian ideal, but Philips' main achievement was to procure a particularly talented manager, George Lee, for his cotton mill.

Entrepreneurs spanned the normal spectrum of human behaviour: there were likely to be individuals with exceptional qualities, as there had always been; but in the past the rewards, whether material or psychic, from warfare, exploration or political intrigue had been greater than those from industry and now the reverse was true for many people.

A shortage of heroes did not matter, because one does not need heroes for either invention or innovation. Invention and prompt innovation offered the prospect of locking in superprofits through a favourable market position. A lot of businessmen were going to find it too risky, but a number were going to be tempted by the potential rewards. Innovation fits into a standard neo-classical framework in which businessmen turned to profit opportunities when these were offered. These opportunities might have been quite transient, but if there were enough businessmen, and enough capital, they should still have been sufficient. And in a world of frequent macroinventions, profit opportunities in practice were substantial in both numbers and scope. In this interpretation, it was the volume, rather than the quality, of entrepreneurship which was crucial. Julian Hoppitt has used bankruptcy figures to give some measure of this volume on the grounds that, although bankruptcy indicates ultimate failure, it is a proxy for those who were willing to have a go. During the eighteenth century there were 33,000 bankruptcies in England, with a marked upward shift from 1760; over half of all bankruptcies in the century occurred after 1770. While bankrupts could be found in all trades and industries, because the growing economy offered wide opportunities, there were particularly sharp increases in rapidly growing industries such as cotton. This shows that there were numerous businessmen who responded to the perceived rewards of innovation; it also suggests that risk increased in a more dynamic economic environment, which is exactly what one would expect because rapid change increased uncertainty, while the increased take-up of credit to finance expansion led to greater instability.

Historians have identified various influences on the supply of businessmen. Britain was already a market economy with a high proportion of the population in the service sector, accustomed to trade and to utilising their capital flexibly. François Crouzet's study of 226 large industrialists between 1750 and 1850 finds that 23 per cent came from mercantile families, 19 per cent from manufacturing families (excluding the sons of managers and craftsmen), and 19 per cent from farming backgrounds – and, of course, farmers in Britain were much more market-orientated than in most countries. Coming from such backgrounds, potential businessmen would probably have had useful personal contacts, easier access to credit and some pre-existing knowledge of business.

This business environment was one contrast between Britain and Continental countries. Another contrast with France, Britain's chief manufacturing rival, was the French government's constant need for loans which, when combined with the country's lack of an efficient capital market, meant that money was raised through such expedients as the sale of offices of profit, which offered attractive returns and opportunities for profitable speculation. It has been suggested that, because of this, French entrepreneurial impulses were more easily diverted into what economists call rent-seeking, that is the acquisition of income which is not earned through labour or the productive use of capital. This is an ingenious idea, but it only focuses on a part of the problem for France, whose larger problem was its limited initial supply of both capital and businessmen. Britain was able to satisfy its government's own substantial need for loans largely from London savings, leaving other businessmen the opportunity for entrepreneurial activity financed by their own profits or by provincial savings and credit. As a result, more people were available to take advantage of the profit opportunities opened up by macro- and microinventions, by new products and by the increasing size of the market. So inventions quickly diffused and, in order to finance these, investment rose too.

All these factors were aided by Britain's political and legal stability. This is often adduced as positive for industrialisation but, as always, we need to specify precisely the mechanisms by which it acted. One possible effect, already mentioned, was the ability of the government to raise money easily and cheaply, thus discouraging the diversion of entrepreneurial energy into rent-seeking. Stability had other benefits. Security on private debt instruments such as mortgages and bills was enhanced, keeping down interest rates in two different ways: by encouraging saving as opposed to hoarding, and by reducing lenders' need to charge a risk premium. Investors in turn not only borrowed money at relatively low interest rates, but also ran a very low risk that their capital assets might be destroyed by military action or civil disorder. Competition was rarely hindered by unnecessary monopolies: these had been frowned on by the common law since the seventeenth century and the government itself kept clear of industry or trade, excepting naval dockyards and the provision of a reasonably efficient postal service. On the other hand, the patent system did provide an important incentive to invention by giving inventors a temporary monopoly. As suggested, however, this could have worked better, and so the government's inaction should not be seen through too rose-tinted spectacles. An interest in education might have been beneficial to economic growth, while, as Chapter 7 will show, the chaos of local government was detrimental to welfare. The government's foreign policy and defence role also had implications for industrialisation, which will be discussed in the next chapter.

Political stability was useful but many countries enjoyed political stability for much of the eighteenth century and did not have an industrial revolution. Successful invention and innovation depended on other things: in particular the opportunities for successful learning-by-doing, and the possibility of earning superprofits from a favourable market position, which in turn was fostered by a large market and, for inventors, the chance of obtaining a patent. A large number of people willing to engage in such activity helped but it is not necessary to suppose that many of them had extraordinary entrepreneurial talents.

Further reading

The essential books for patents and invention are C. MacLeod, *Inventing the Industrial Revolution: The English Patent System 1660–1800* (Cambridge, 1988) and H.I. Dutton, *The Patent System and Inventive Activity during the Industrial Revolution, 1750–1852* (Manchester, 1984); Dutton's 'economic man' citation is from p. 108 and the quotation from Watt from *ibid*. p. 109. For a theoretical basis to patents and innovation, including the idea of 'knowledge capital', see G. Grossman and E. Helpmann, *Invention and Growth in the Global Economy* (Cambridge, Mass. 1991) and A. Young's article (see Chapter 1). MacLeod's 'Strategies for innovation: the diffusion of new technology in nineteenth-century British industry', *EcHR*, 45 (1992), pp. 285–307 sets out the continued incentive for firms to invent; Gillian Cookson's 'Family firms and business networks: textile engineering in

Yorkshire, 1780–1830', *Business History*, 39 (1997), pp. 1–20 outlines a more cooperative model but the two are not incompatible since firms' behaviour will differ in different circumstances. J.R. Harris's works on skill (see Chapter 3) are essential for learning-by-doing and human capital; see especially the final chapter of *Industrial Espionage*; also D. Jeremy, *Transatlantic Industrial Revolution: The Diffusion of Textile Technologies between Britain and America 1790–1830* (Oxford, 1981). P.K. O'Brien, 'Mainsprings of technical progress in Europe 1750–1850' in P. Mathias and J. Davies, *Innovation and Technology in Europe from the 18th Century to the Present Day* (Oxford, 1991) contains a succinct criticism of attempts to link demand with innovation. For N.F.R. Crafts' original article see Chapter 1; also see other references in that chapter and his 'Macroinventions, economic growth and "industrial revolution" in Britain and France', *EcHR*, 48 (1995), pp. 591–8 and D. Landes, 'Some further thoughts on accident in history: a reply to Professor Crafts', *Ibid.*, pp. 599–601. For comparative material on patent systems C. MacLeod, 'The paradoxes of patenting: invention and its diffusion in eighteenth- and nineteenth-century Britain, France and North America', *Technology and Culture*, 32 (1991), pp. 885–910. French technology is a puzzle: MacLeod suggests that the French state was supportive of both invention and innovation, but R. Briggs, 'The Académie Royale des Sciences and the pursuit of utility', *Past and Present*, 131 (1991), pp. 38–88 reinforces Harris's points about French backwardness in many areas. The absurd quotation about potty-training is taken from R. Lewis and A. Maude, *The English Middle Classes* (1949), citing E. Jones, *Papers on Psycho-analysis* (1923), p. 694.

H. Catling, 'The evolution of spinning' in J.G. Jenkins, *The Wool Textile Industry in Great Britain* (1972).

R.H. Clapperton, *The Paper-Making Machine: Its Invention, Evolution and Development* (Oxford, 1967).

F. Crouzet, *The First Industrialists: The Problem of Origins* (1985).

D. Greasley and L. Oxley, 'Endogenous growth' (see Chapter 1).

J.R. Harris, *The British Iron Industry 1700–1850* (1988).

J. Hoppitt, *Risk and Failure in English Business 1700–1800* (Cambridge, 1987).

C.K. Hyde, *Technological Change and the British Iron Industry 1700–1870* (Guildford, 1977).

P.K. O'Brien, 'The micro-foundations of macro invention: the case of the Reverend Edmund Cartwright', *Textile History*, 28 (1997), pp. 201–33.

W. Rubinstein, *Men of Property: The Very Wealthy in Britain since the Industrial Revolution* (1981).

G.N. von Tunzelmann, *Steam Power and Industrialisation to 1860* (Oxford, 1978).

A.P. Wadsworth and J.L. de Mann, *The Cotton Trade and Industrial Lancashire 1600–1780* (Manchester, 1931).

Chapter 6

Market size and integration

Up to now market size has been considered primarily in relation to invention, but Adam Smith emphasised the advantages of a large market because of the potential it offered for the division of labour: 'Smithian growth'. Market size depended on the effective integration of local markets into regional markets, and of these into a national market which in turn could be integrated internationally. All these processes, particularly national and international integration, were heavily influenced by transport change. These topics, and their relationship to the process of industrialisation, form the agenda for this chapter.

Regional development

Discussion of industrial regions is bedevilled by definitional problems since even geographers, who ought to know, cannot agree on what constitutes a region. Here regions will be taken as continuous land areas in which the inputs to economic activities were largely homogeneous and the outputs related to each other in some way. Even with such a definition, however, it is convenient to let convention override it to some extent. Lancashire and Cheshire, Yorkshire and the East Midlands together formed a continuous area in which inputs included waterpower and local coal, and outputs textiles and engineering goods, but conventionally they are treated as separate regions. On the other hand, London had an enormous diversity of outputs but is always regarded as a region. It should also be noted that, with the exception of London, conventional British regions used for statistical aggregation all contain large agricultural areas and thus regional statistics do not indicate the true extent of change in industrialising areas.

Before coal became an important source of energy, industry was dispersed. Fast-flowing water, as the most reliable power source before the days of steam, was important for industries which used simple powered machinery, such as milling, the fulling of cloth, and ironworking. However, other locational factors mattered. These included access to water routes, since water was the cheapest means of transport. Proximity to centres of consumption, which in practice meant location in towns, was desirable for most small-scale consumer goods industries. Textiles were different: as the industrial goods which even the poor bought, they were the first mass-market product, meaning one in which both production and consumption were on a large scale. The large quantities involved made it worthwhile to incur the additional transaction costs involved in organising production in areas remote from the products' final destinations or even from their raw material supplies. It was also important that textiles had a high value in relation to their bulk, since transport costs were usually the most important single component of transaction costs. The areas to which textile manufacture moved were the areas of proto-industry, usually marked by surplus rural labour and the lack of other industrial occupations, although there were many deviations from this ideal type.

A final important constraint on location was raw material supply. Raw materials included wood, a necessary ingredient for iron-smelting before coal was used; iron and other metals; and coal itself. Coal was already used by the mid-eighteenth century in various industrial activities such as glass-making and working wrought iron (as opposed to smelting iron from ore), and for domestic heating. Its use rose dramatically and continuously after that date. Coal substituted for wood in the smelting of iron and in its further conversion to wrought iron, and via the medium of the steam engine, coal came increasingly into use to provide power, replacing wind, water, horses and human beings; although before 1830 or so the cost advantages of steam power were small and its progress was quite slow. As coal is a heavy commodity in relation to its value, its price was substantially affected by transport costs and therefore it is not surprising that much industry became clustered around the coalfields. Coal could be transported cheaply by sea,

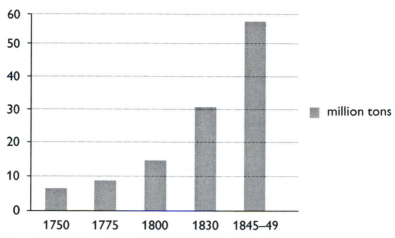

Figure 6.1 Coal production (after Table 6.1)

and with rather greater expense by inland waterway or, later, by rail: so seaports also had reasonably cheap coal supplies, while there was a major incentive to improve inland transport networks.

A simple model of regional development, therefore, would portray the diverse influences on location of the mid-eighteenth century being increasingly superseded by the influence of coal. And what applied to regions also applied to individual industries. Since Britain's coal needed fewer inputs of capital and labour to extract than most foreign coal, Britain had a huge comparative advantage in coal-using industries. These were, in particular, the metal-smelting and metal-working industries: iron, machinery production, and from the 1830s, railway engineering. Highly mechanised industries such as textiles also used substantial amounts of coal in steam engines by the early nineteenth century, although it was not as large a component in production costs as it was for the other industries mentioned above. While textile areas which were not situated on coalfields declined, those that remained increasingly specialised in producing different types of textile. The simple model of location, in which coal is the only significant factor, could be supplemented in order to explain this specialisation by adding the effects of economies of scale, accumulation of human capital and linkages to other industries.

We can hypothesise that certain branches of the textile industry were established in particular areas initially because of minor locational advantages or simply by chance. Their existence encouraged the formation of firms specialising in ancillary activities. The proximity of such firms enhanced the attraction of these locations to new entrants in the original branch of the industry and thus a dynamic expansion took place. At the same time, the increasing division of labour made possible by size encouraged the efficient accumulation of human capital, thus adding a further locational benefit for those firms already established and for new ones. It also became economic to increase the density of infrastructural projects such as roads and canals. Such groups of related firms are sometimes called clusters, firms in clusters gaining beneficial externalities from each other's proximity. Linkages to other industries could be both backward and forward; the former refers to the demands which any industry places on its suppliers. Thus factory textile production stimulated demand for chemicals for bleaching and dyeing, machinery, transport services and building products for both factories and workers' housing. Forward linkages are those in which the product itself becomes an input for some other product. The most notable forward linkage, already discussed, was that from coal to many other industries. Coal and iron together constituted the main inputs into heavy engineering production, such as iron castings for building construction, rails and locomotives. In each of the main textile regions, the concentration of the textile preparatory processes through to spinning and weaving can be seen as the manifestation of a series of forward linkages from one to the other.

A map of industrial Britain in 1850 is therefore very different from one of 1750, although there were important continuities. In 1750 textiles were the main industry, mainly woollens but also linen and silk, and to a lesser extent cotton. East Anglia was a big textile producer, as was the West Country – Devon, Somerset, Wiltshire and Gloucestershire. Textiles were also important in the East Midlands/ Lancashire-Cheshire/ Yorkshire triangle (henceforth 'the triangle') and in Lowland Scotland. In all these textile production was largely dispersed in the homes or workshops of spinners and weavers, in some variant of proto-industrialisation. The northeast's main product was coal, much of this being sent by sea to London, and cheap coal also made it the major glass-making region. Coal was also mined in the West Midlands and used in the region's numerous forges in which small metal goods of all kinds such as nails, locks, buckles, guns and ornaments were produced. It was also an iron-making region while in its outlier, the Shropshire coal area, the Darbys were achieving their breakthrough in coke iron production. The Lancashire and Yorkshire regions were also emerging as coal and metal producers, both of primary metals, particularly Sheffield steel, and of products such as files, which were essential for the precision shaping of metal components. North Staffordshire, geographically in the North Midlands although in fact as close to Lancashire-Cheshire as to the East and West Midlands, was becoming important as a pottery producer. An important if small industrial region was Cornwall and West Devon, producing copper and tin and already a user of steam engines for drainage. Much iron was still produced in small wood-rich areas, barely deserving the term regions, such as the Forest of Dean and the Furness district. Finally, London produced an enormous variety of goods: much low-value production, especially of textiles, had gone elsewhere but it was a centre of craft production, from carriages and clocks to clothing; many of these trades also had a volume production side which relied on a detailed division of labour while there were also highly capitalised batch or flow production industries such as brewing and sugar-refining.

By 1850 proto-industrialisation as a system of production had shrunk, surviving mainly as forms of outwork in partially mechanised or unmechanised consumer goods industries such as foot-wear, lace- and glove-making, and in big city clothing industries. The East Anglian and West Country textile industries had been reduced to relative insignificance, with mainly specialist producers surviving in scattered islands of industry. In the regions of the triangle textiles were still king, having grown enormously from 1750 on and become predominantly factory-based. Within these the East Midlands, the early centre of Arkwright's activities, had reverted to its original specialisation in hosiery and lace, while Lancashire specialised in cottons and Yorkshire in woollens and worsteds. These regions had also diversified industrially. Coal production had grown rapidly as had, from the late eighteenth century, engineering, beginning with textile machinery but expanding to include machine-tools, stationary steam engines and later railway locomotives. The chemicals and glass industries were particularly strong in Lancashire-Cheshire, while in Yorkshire,

Sheffield steel and its products such as cutlery were increasingly important. With its cheap coal, the northeast added chemicals and engineering to its glass industry, although its role as an iron and steel producer and iron shipbuilding region lay largely in the future. Lowland Scotland had also diversified: textiles remained important but it had also become a centre of coal and iron production and there was a wide range of miscellaneous industries, such as tobacco processing, distilling and paper-making. The West Midlands had diversified much less: coal and iron production had increased although its Shropshire outlier, the cradle of coke-iron manufacture, was now of little importance; the region was still most notable as a producer of small metal goods, mainly in workshop-type trades, although on a much larger scale than before. In South Wales too, diversification was limited; it had burgeoned as a coal and iron producer in the late eighteenth century but competition from Scotland had reduced the relative importance of iron by 1850 and it was beginning to focus more and more on coalmining. Of the smaller industrial regions, Cornwall continued as a tin and copper producer because of the presence of these metals in the region, but the small iron-producing regions that relied on wood for fuel had sunk into obscurity. Finally, London remained the largest single industrial city with an even wider range of consumer goods industries as consumption increased, and with an important foothold in engineering.

Many of these locational changes – and continuities – can be accounted for by the influences on location described earlier. The diversification which the regions of the triangle experienced, for instance, stemmed in part from the textile industry itself, which put heavy demands on the machinery and chemicals industries. These in turn expanded, creating external economies and facilitating the growth of human capital. The subsequent development of machine tool production and railway engineering was not a direct linkage from textiles but built upon these external economies and on human capital accumulation within the engineering industry, together with the regions' coal. The relative lack of diversification of South Wales can be accounted for partly by mining's lack of backward linkages. Machinery was little used except for the winding and pumping gear at the pit-head: transport was necessary but locomotives, waggons and so on for railways often came from outside: their production was facilitated by human capital which had accumulated more in regions where engineering was already established. The northeast, with a long tradition of deep mining and therefore some engineering expertise, was better placed than South Wales to diversify even though it lacked, in this period, native iron. Lowland Scotland differed from the regions of the triangle in that it had a large iron industry which was based on favourable raw material supplies. Like the northeast it was to develop iron shipbuilding and heavy engineering, but in 1850 their growth lay largely in the future. Finally, London depended largely on its huge consumer market which facilitated economies of scale and human capital development; linkages were mainly between the subdivided branches of individual industries, such as the many different trades which made London a centre of coach and carriage production.

It is less easy to explain why Lancashire-Cheshire and Yorkshire overtook the other textile regions in the first place. Development in the East Midlands, the least famous of the big textile regions, can be explained because it had long been a centre of hosiery manufacture and Arkwright's first factories were established to provide yarn for this industry. But there was not a huge difference in the scale of production between different textile regions in 1750, so economies of scale cannot have been a factor in Lancashire's and Yorkshire's initial rise to prominence. These two regions' wage levels may have been lower in 1750, but that soon changed. Waterpower for factories became important from the 1770s, which increased their competitive advantage over East Anglia, although not so much over the West Country. It has also been suggested that West Country workers, in an older-established industry with, in the early days, a more capitalistic organisation than the north, were more resistant to technical change. With the advent of coal as a significant power source, the supremacy of the regions of the triangle becomes more or less self-evident, but this did not occur until after 1800, by which time their dominance was well established.

Whatever the reasons for the rise of textiles in these regions, the concentrated nature of the industry, when combined with the availability of coal, was very important in subsequent regional development. The other coal-rich regions could not become textile centres because they lacked the requisite external economies and human capital. Attempts to establish factory textile industries outside the established regions were never, in the long run, successful. The importance of textiles was the number of linkages it had to other industries, as compared with coal or iron by themselves. As a result, the triangle developed other major industries such as chemicals and engineering. Pre-factory textiles, however, had no such linkages and so East Anglia, whose industry declined in the late eighteenth and early nineteenth centuries, had no replacement and became deindustrialised. Intermediate was the West Country, particularly Gloucestershire where there was waterpower and some coal. Its textile industry was not large enough to enjoy the external economies of Yorkshire, the main woollen region, and hence suffered economic deprivation from the 1820s as competitive pressures sharpened. But more specialist producers survived and, as the industry had continued on a substantial scale into the age of machinery, a local engineering industry developed.

Service industries as well as manufacturing experienced locational pressures. Transport was a major service which grew in part as a result of backward linkages from the development of large-scale mining and manufacturing. In turn, transport provided backward linkages. From land transport these were largely to construction – of roads, canals and later railways – while there were also strong linkages from railways to coal, iron and engineering; linkages to service industries were largely to diffuse if important activities such as the provision of stabling for the ubiquitous horse, and blacksmithing for its shoes and for the metal components of carts and coaches. The linkages from sea transport included more concentrated services such as docks and warehousing, as well as virtually new industries such as insurance. Once these were established, economies of scale were likely to act with the same force as in manufacturing. Firms and workers would develop expertise; the increasing division of labour would reduce the cost of training; and transaction costs would fall as the volume of transactions rose. Therefore a model of service industry location would see such industries developing strongly in seaports, particularly those engaging in long-distance trade in which the demand for insurance and warehousing was likely to be strongest. While there was likely to be some concentration of other service activities such as banking, due to economies of scale, a simple model does not provide many pointers as to where this would have occurred, except that some services were likely to flourish in transport centres of any kind.

Transport

Transport growth was more than just a backward linkage from trade and industrial development. Innovation in transport has been seen as important, by some as all-important, to industrialisation.

It is a truism that pre-industrial Britain's transport network was already much better than that of most European countries. Britain has a lengthy and indented sea-coast, a valuable asset since transport by water was, in ideal conditions, far cheaper than transport by land. Britain has one mile (1.6 km) of coastline for every 55 square miles (141 square km) of land area compared with France's ratio of 1:134. Britain is not blessed with long navigable rivers but some navigation is possible on the Severn and Thames which penetrate the most landlocked regions: the Midlands and south. In the late seventeenth and early eighteenth centuries improvements to other rivers had established river navigations which had considerable local value. However, the availability of sea transport was much more important to inter-regional trade, with the flow of northeastern coal to London the most important example. London could also secure grain and hay from a wide area around the coasts of East Anglia and southern England. In return coastal shipping distributed imported goods and local manufactures from London. Bristol, Hull, Liverpool and Glasgow also performed, on a smaller scale, the same functions.

Although detailed productivity calculations for miscellaneous coastal trades are probably impossible to make, study of the northeast to London coal trade suggests that total factor productivity (see Appendix) could have doubled between the early eighteenth and the early nineteenth centuries. The figures are highly uncertain but all scholars agree that there was some increase. There was no one reason for this. Shipowners' expertise improved and their scale of operations increased as there was a move away from fragmented ship ownership towards specialised shipping firms. Capital investment in harbours and loading and unloading facilities, together with small-scale technical innovation, sharply increased productivity in port. Better charts and information for captains also helped, as did the provision of navigational aids such as lighthouses. Some of the improvement seems to have been simply due to reduced manning without significant technical change in the ships themselves – steamships were not introduced until the mid-nineteenth century. In general the reasons for productivity increase can be categorised as a mixture of external economies and specialisation, both in large part resulting from the increased volume of trade; learning-by-doing; increased capital input; and a small amount of technical change.

Britain's road network, even before turnpikes, was better than it has often been given credit for. A surge of bridge-building in medieval times was testimony to the considerable volume of inland trade in Britain at an early date. These bridges and the existing parish roads almost certainly provided a better transport network than existed on most of the Continent, and there were regular carrying services by 1700. Early examples of turnpikes existed in the 1700s but it was only around 1750 that their development took off, with mileage quadrupling from around 3,400 (5,500 km) to over 13,000 (21,000 km) by 1770. At the same time a renewed phase of bridge-building began. By the late eighteenth century it is estimated that England had the same mileage of good roads as France, with one quarter of the land area.

An empty road is of no economic use. What made turnpikes valuable was their role in reducing the cost of carriage and speeding it up. Dorian Gerhold has shown that, as well as turnpikes, a number of different factors entered into this cost reduction. As trade and carrying services slowly expanded, there were economies of scale of various kinds – for instance, larger firms could cut the costs of fodder purchase. In the late eighteenth century there were big improvements in animal breeding, resulting in horses which were both stronger and ate less; this seems tough on the horses but contributed to economic efficiency. Over the period coach design improved, enabling more passengers to be carried. Turnpikes' contribution was in part passive – the ability to levy tolls provided an institutional mechanism which enabled the funds for road maintenance to at least keep pace with traffic increase. The active contribution of turnpike trustees and engineers was the building of completely new roads and cut-offs, the reduction of gradients, and from the late eighteenth century the improvement of surfaces; the last was achieved through developments in surfacing methods which could have been used on other roads but were much more likely to be used on turnpikes which, through tolls, secured a return on their expenditure. These improvements were long-term rather than sudden and so the idea of turnpikes was not a radical invention which offered a completely new method of cost reduction. Rather, they were an innovation which diffused in response to perceived demand. There was no sudden rise in demand around 1750, but the market had grown to a point at which existing traffic warranted substantial investment in turnpikes. In turn, these brought down costs and stimulated further traffic growth.

As with coastal shipping, the result of these various forces for improvement in road transport was a substantial fall in costs. Gerhold estimates that total factor productivity in long-distance goods carriage doubled between the end of the seventeenth century and the early nineteenth century, increasing still more by the dawn of the railway age in the 1830s. The productivity of coaches for passenger carriage increased to a similar extent. In addition, regularity and speed for goods and, even more, for passengers increased markedly.

The effects of improvements in speed and regularity were very important even if, unlike cost reductions, they are almost impossible to measure. One small but important example was noted in Chapter 5: a reduction in the expense and difficulty of gaining patents because of easier travel to London. Owners and managers of businesses spent less time in travelling to oversee their sales operations so had more time to devote to improving productive efficiency. All sorts of commercial transactions were facilitated by the improvements. For instance, in the late eighteenth century commercial enterprises often cut out a layer of middlemen in the sales process by starting up their own commercial travellers: Charles Dickens' 'bagmen'. Road carriage charges were still too expensive to allow heavy goods to be economically carried any great distance, but high-value commodities could economically travel a long way by road. In the 1790s Peter Stubs, a Warrington file manufacturer, paid around three shillings (15p) for a hundredweight (51 kilos) of high-grade steel to be carried the fifty miles or so from Sheffield. This was just 5 per cent of the steel's value. Security of carriage was increased as carrying firms grew larger and could carry goods over longer distances, rather than passing them from carrier to carrier.

For the carriage of heavy goods, canals provided one solution; it was only partial because canals had many limitations. One fundamental obstacle was the cost of building them, which meant that traffic had to be substantial to make them pay. This helps to explain why it was only from the late 1760s that canals began to be developed in a big way. Like turnpikes, they involved no major innovation but diffused in response to perceived traffic levels and hence profitability. Their cost also limited their geographical coverage: few canals were built specifically to serve rural areas, and in hilly areas canals became much more expensive and therefore potentially less viable. Hence in the northeast waggonways – horse-drawn railways – were extensively used; their operating costs were higher than those of canals, but they were cheaper to build and thus viable at lower traffic levels.

Although canals' operating costs were much less than those of roads, sea transport remained cheaper. Therefore canals were not arteries for long-distance trade in heavy commodities – these still tended to flow towards ports and complete their journey by sea. Canals reduced transport costs for long-distance carriage of higher-value commodities, but this was only significant when there was a reasonably direct route. Their most important effect was to cut transport costs sharply in localised areas, particularly Lancashire, the West Midlands and South Wales, and to some extent Yorkshire and the East Midlands. Because of the very high cost of carrying coal in relation to its value, the extension of coal-using industries was limited without water transport. Such industries needed to locate as near as possible to pit-heads, but this might involve high costs in transporting their other raw materials and difficulties in getting labour. It also meant that high-cost coal-fields and individual pits had local monopolies because lack of transport choked off competition from elsewhere. Pit-head prices of coal in South Yorkshire and the Midlands around 1800 varied from two shillings and sixpence per ton (12p per tonne) to over nine shillings per ton (44p per tonne). Variations in quality make exact comparisons difficult but it is clear that road carriage had less impact on local monopolies than canal carriage. In the 1790s Peter Stubs paid around one shilling per ton mile (*c.* 3p per tonne km) for his carriage, while the Leeds–London route was around nine old pence per ton (*c.* 2.3p per tonne kilometre), no doubt because there was some discount for distance. By comparison canal carriage for a bulk cargo such as coal was, in 1790, around 1.5 old pence per ton mile or less (*c.* 0.4p per tonne kilometre). By breaking local monopolies and widening the area in which cheap coal was available, canals also widened the area in which coal could be used in industry. Thus in 1750 coal from the high-cost Warwickshire coalfield cost 50 shillings per ton (£2.45 per tonne) in landlocked Northampton, most of this being transport cost. The improvement of the river Nene in 1761 opened the market to Newcastle coal; in spite of a much greater distance, by sea and river navigation, coal prices fell to 35 shillings per ton (£1.72 per tonne). The opening of the Grand Junction canal in the 1790s further reduced the price to 20 shillings per ton (98p per tonne). In spite of such reductions, however, it is evident that coal prices were still much higher off the coalfields.

Transport change was the final ingredient in the forces for regional specialisation outlined earlier. It did not eliminate the cost benefit of locating power- or heat-using industries on coalfields, but enabled the coalfield regions to greatly widen their market for the secondary products – iron, textiles, engineering products – in which they specialised.

Improvements in long-distance sea transport, particularly in the colonial trade, were also important. Chapter 4 discussed the growth of the American market for exports; one reason why it grew so much was improvement in the productivity of shipping, and hence a fall in its cost. As with other improvements in transport productivity, much of this was due not to radical technical change but to the improvement of public goods such as defence, to economies of scale and to learning-by-doing. Britain's growing hegemony over the oceans reduced the threat from privateers and pirates so that merchantmen needed to carry fewer guns and hence smaller crews. In wartime, the organisational innovation of the convoy system helped to retain this advantage. As the American trade grew larger, various economies of scale became available. A simple and startling example is the reduction of average port time in the Chesapeake from 100 to 50 days between 1700 and 1770. Because of the greater volume of trade, ships had to wait less time while a suitable cargo was assembled. Packing became more efficient: tobacco, for instance, was packed more tightly into larger containers – an example of learning-by-doing.

The growth of ocean commerce led to greater specialisation and economies of scale in British ports, leading to further reductions in shipping costs. Port improvements in the late eighteenth and early nineteenth centuries were particularly marked in towns specialising in long-distance trade, due to its rapid growth. London and Liverpool, for example, saw massive dock-building in this period. In Liverpool the area of docks doubled to around 25 acres (10 hectares) between 1785 and 1796; in London the West India Docks, costing over £1 million, were opened in 1802 with accommodation for over 600 vessels; the even more expensive London Docks opened in 1805 and the East India Docks in 1806. The growth of marine insurance was held back to some extent as, apart from the Lloyds insurance market in which wealthy individuals acted collectively to underwrite risks, there were only two chartered companies. However, private underwriting developed in provincial ports and in the late eighteenth century shipowners established mutual insurance clubs which burgeoned rapidly. The development of insurance, both in shipping and in other sectors of the economy, reduced risk; this encouraged new entrants and allowed existing firms to increase the scale of their activities.

Market size and integration

The increase in the size of the market was caused partly by the growth of colonial trade as discussed in Chapter 4. This growth was based on population increase which took advantage of virtually free land. There was also a gradual increase in the size of the domestic market, based in part on higher living standards made possible by the low food prices of the first half of the eighteenth century. The home population also grew from around 1730 on, although slowly at first. As discussed in Chapter 4, this is more problematic in terms of its effect on aggregate demand, because of the likelihood of diminishing returns; up to around 1780, however, it is likely that the domestic population increase had a mildly beneficial effect, since it brought previously underexploited land into use. Finally, transport improvements integrated local and regional markets in Britain and thus the market conditions for firms in favoured regions changed.

All these changes pushed out the demand curves faced by individual firms. The relevant changes were primarily the growth in American trade, and later other export trades, and the integration of markets; the growth of the aggregate domestic market was too slow to have any significant impact.

Because of growing integration, firms in low-cost regions enjoyed a much larger market. In these circumstances firms could, if they wished, have pushed up prices and would still have sold the same quantity of goods. If they had done so, however, the consequent supernormal profits would have attracted new entrants and prices would have fallen. Alternatively, low-cost firms could have aggressively invaded new markets and reduced prices immediately. Whichever course of action was taken, a one-off increase in real incomes would have taken place as consumer prices declined. However, the importance of these influences was that they were more or less continuous. Continuous effects meant that demand curves were constantly shifting and that therefore there were permanent incentives for firms in favoured industries and regions to expand. Growing export demand, compounded by the fall in shipping costs, would have had a similar effect on firms in export industries.

The mechanism outlined above, and its dynamic effects, have been highlighted by Rick Szostak. As the industries of favoured regions grew, scale effects and the benefits of specialisation improved their efficiency and lowered their costs still further. The iron industry shows these processes at work. In the initial stages of coke-smelting, rapid expansion was held back by a lack of skilled labour; by 1775 this shortage was remedied by migration and on-the-job training. However, transport costs meant that regional monopolies in coke iron production still persisted, for instance in the Shropshire and Black Country areas of the West Midlands. By the late eighteenth century, however, low-cost Welsh iron was taking over 'neutral' markets such as London and reducing the ability of producers elsewhere to set prices autonomously, although national prices were by no means equalised. The fairly roundabout nature of transhipment from Wales, which first required a journey to the coast, did not help. From 1830 onwards the combination of cheap Scottish iron, which added to competitive pressures, and railways, which further reduced transport costs, finally eroded regional monopolies. Iron producers in less favoured regions, however, had experienced a long period before this in which profit margins had been under threat and local producers had had to become more efficient to survive. Welsh and later Scottish producers, conversely, had reaped superprofits which had both attracted capital into the industry and had also financed the rapid expansion of existing firms such as the huge Cyfartha works in South Wales.

Market integration benefits were not just evident in a rapidly growing industry such as iron. Tobacco, used in pipes, for chewing and as snuff, was a well-established consumer goods industry. Bristol had been a major force in the industry but in the late eighteenth and early nineteenth centuries the tobacco trade grew rapidly in London and Liverpool. With falling transport costs, Bristol firms could take advantage of the more efficient London and Liverpool docks and obtain tobacco leaf more cheaply at these ports than at Bristol itself. On the other hand, cheaper transport also meant that Liverpool and London manufacturers could compete in regions served by all three cities, such as the Midlands, and this drove down wholesale prices.

On neo-classical assumptions, constraints attended the supply-side response to autonomous demand growth. The response was restricted because labour and capital came from existing occupations, and their diversion would have diminished output in these, even if there had been a net gain in national income due to gains from trade and economies of scale. The extent to which these constraints applied to export trades was discussed in Chapter 4, and they would apply in the same way to the increase of exports caused by a decline in shipping costs. In the case of internal market integration, such constraints lost much of their force. There was, initially, no net gain in aggregate national demand and so the possibilities of non-inflationary readjustment of resources were much greater. Capital and labour could flow into expanding industries in favoured regions both from agriculture, and also from similar industries in less favoured regions. Conversely, the decline of industries in less favoured regions freed resources for agriculture or other uses. There were limits on the rapid movement of all these factors as suggested in Chapters 2 and 3. Nevertheless it is notable how, in the iron industry, skilled workers were willing to move long distances to form the nucleus of a workforce; thus the South Wales industry drew on workers from the Birmingham area. Capital in the industry also moved inter-regionally and, in periods of high prices, flowed in from outside the industry. At times of rapid expansion this may have been sourced partly from credit and may thus have been potentially inflationary. Schumpeter's treatment of credit creation seems appropriate here: it might cause temporary and local inflations but eventually a fall in prices would occur as supply increased.

The efficiency benefits of market integration were not confined to the realisation of lower raw material costs and scale benefits, which Szostak highlighted. Harvey Leibenstein's concept of X-efficiency is also relevant. Leibenstein's insight was that firms operate at different levels of efficiency so their total costs are not just determined by differing raw material costs and wages. Efficiency differences could occur for many reasons: a firm might have a cheap raw material supply which allowed it to get away with inefficiency in other respects; a diversified firm or a wealthy family might have a number of interests, some of which might be so profitable that others could be allowed to operate inefficiently and unprofitably; or a local monopoly might allow a firm to pass on the costs of its inefficiency to consumers. The idea of X-efficiency challenges the neo-classical assumption that businessmen are profit-maximisers. There is, however, plenty of empirical evidence for X-efficiency differences, and the notion accords with most people's intuitive conviction that human capacities are as variable as individuals are more or less hardworking, intelligent and able to respond to challenges. X-efficiency will vary from firm to firm, but the less the competitive pressure the greater the likelihood that potential levels of X-efficiency will not be achieved.

The integration of markets meant that firms were faced, not only with competition from other firms in regions with lower raw material costs and/or scale economies, but also with growing pressure from firms elsewhere which had achieved higher levels of X-efficiency. This might offer a solution to the conundrum that the regions of the triangle emerged as dominant in textile production before steam power made a significant impact. Szostak has suggested that they may have been lower-cost producers prior to 1750, but their advantage over other regions was muted until transport costs fell, allowing these regions to quickly overtake others. A further – speculative – suggestion is that these lower costs were the result of generic regional advantages in X-efficiency, perhaps resulting from different institutional arrangements which were already in place before mid-century. Even if this suggestion is unwarranted, it seems certain that the integration of markets would have improved X-efficiency throughout the economy. Leibenstein considers that, in modern economies, the improvement of

X-efficiency is the main benefit flowing from the removal of barriers to trade such as tariffs. The usual rationale for such removal is that it improves allocative efficiency: the allocation of resources to their most appropriate use, enabling the realisation of gains from trade. In our period, when barriers to trade were largely the internal ones of transport cost, it seems likely that the allocative gains were greater because of the enormous advantages flowing from the integration into the national economy of regions with cheap coal and iron. In spite of these caveats, X-efficiency gains must have been made and may have been important. Their great advantage for economic growth is that their achievement would not have involved the addition of much capital or labour – on the contrary, efficiency gains should release these factors – so they were not liable to be inhibited by the constraints outlined above.

The argument that market size is likely to be correlated with inventive activity was discussed in Chapter 5. In itself, the acceleration of invention was the single most important aspect of the process of integration discussed in this chapter. Nevertheless the process of breaking down regional monopolies does help to explain what was almost equally important: the diffusion of inventions, that is innovation.

Innovations in transport were directly related to the size of the market. As elsewhere, the argument risks circularity – transport changes increased market size which caused transport changes – so needs careful analysis. In particular, the initial causes of increased market size should lie outside the system. As discussed in Chapter 2, there is strong evidence that decisions to build both turnpikes and canals depended on the amount of traffic that was anticipated. Since their technology was not new, this suggests that traffic levels had increased in the early eighteenth century up to a point where turnpikes became viable; canals came somewhat later. This initial increase can be related to rising agricultural and coal output, and a general growth in prosperity, probably caused in the main by improvements in agriculture which lowered food prices. Increased traffic had already led to some economies of scale and consequently some reductions in transport costs even before turnpiking and canal-building. The prior existence of good sea communications and a relatively good road system facilitated this process.

Once transport improvements had started to diffuse in response to the initial rise in demand, they further reduced costs and thus stimulated yet more traffic growth. This led to more economies of scale and learning-by-doing effects in the provision of transport services, again cutting costs. The rise in traffic levels in areas where improvements had been adopted spilt over elsewhere, providing an incentive for their wider diffusion. Finally, the increase in regional specialisation facilitated by cheaper transport itself added to transport demand, so it is possible to construct a dynamic model in which transport improvements act as an agent in their own diffusion. Of course, there were other factors simultaneously at work leading to an increase in traffic levels, notably the process of invention and innovation in the wider economy.

Growing market integration because of transport change then helped to accelerate innovation in other sectors of the economy. It increased competitive pressure, so firms needed to innovate more quickly than they might otherwise have done in order to improve X-efficiency. Innovations in textile machinery, for instance, spread quickly from wherever they were made: the Gloucestershire woollen industry seems to have been willing to innovate as rapidly as Yorkshire, although ultimately it was less successful. Knowledge of innovations was disseminated more quickly by transport improvements, which facilitated the spread of books, newspapers and journals as well as personal contact between inventors and entrepreneurs. Transport improvements also aided labour migration, both the long-distance migration already mentioned and also short-distance movement between different towns. This diffused the knowledge acquired through learning-by-doing, since skilled workmen were often the best repository of particular knacks or the knowledge of how best to operate specific types of machinery. In economic terminology, knowledge capital spillovers were accentuated by transport improvements.

Finally, market integration accelerated innovation via more rapid investment. The rapid growth of favoured regions as a result of transport improvement meant that industrialists in these regions had a Schumpeterian stimulus to rapid investment in order to expand output. Such investment was likely to be in the most up-to-date technology, since there would have been no point in investing in older technology unless it was much cheaper. Since many of the improvements in machinery were directed towards reducing its price, older technology was not likely to be cheaper.

This rapid investment led to concentrations of modern technology. From the late eighteenth century these were notable in
Lancashire cottons and Yorkshire woollens, in the iron industry
generally and especially in South Wales, and in machinery
construction in centres within the triangle. The absolute rate of
innovation was therefore higher in these areas, while the concentration of modern machinery increased the scope for learning-by-
doing.

Important though market integration through transport change
was during the Industrial Revolution, its limits as a factor in growth
should be understood. The initial impetus to invention came
because a sufficient market size had already been reached in mid-
and late eighteenth-century Britain; this happened in part because
of transport improvements which had already taken place. So in
spite of all the important changes of the century after 1750, enough
had already been done to ensure a substantial market. Furthermore
the process of invention, by lowering costs, would itself have
ensured that competitive pressures were exerted on other regions
and thus encouraged innovation. Transport improvements and the
resulting growth in market integration speeded up this process but
did not by themselves cause it.

Regional development and the Industrial Revolution

The differing fortunes of Britain's regions during the Industrial Revolution have led some historians to focus on their significance to the
industrialisation process. There are two main lines of approach.
One, particularly associated with Sidney Pollard, emphasises the
centrality of coal-based regions in the industrialisation process. The
other, associated with a variety of scholars including Bill Rubinstein
and Clive Lee, downgrades the significance of the Industrial Revolution by emphasising the continuities in British economic history,
particularly those provided by the size and economic importance of
London.

The supporters of coal-based industrial regions point to the
importance of linkages within regions; the relative lack of inter-
regional trade in heavy commodities, so that industries which used
coal on a large scale remained localised; the extent to which capital
markets remained localised; and the rapid increase in wages in

industrialised regions and not outside them. The supporters of the centrality and importance of London do not deny the existence of these phenomena but play down their relative importance. They stress the prosperity and commercial importance of Britain before industrialisation, characteristics which were most exemplified in London, which had the highest wage levels and by far the greatest concentrations of wealth. During the Industrial Revolution, London's relative importance within the British economy remained virtually unchanged; wages in some industrial areas grew to near-London levels, but in absolute terms London wages remained high while it and the south together still had the greatest concentration of wealth. On this account, there was an Industrial Revolution but it didn't matter very much.

The biggest problem with both approaches is that they effectively leave aside the question of market size. Lacking this key variable, the regional approach cannot explain invention and innovation, or the ultimate source of each region's income. Market size was vital to inventive activity since profit-seeking invention was costly and therefore depended for its viability on a large market. The diffusion of inventions depended for its effectiveness and speed on the degree of concentration and rapidity of growth of industries, which was also a function of market size. In emphasising linkages within regions, the regional approach misses the essential point that the final output of regions had to be sold outside them: specialised industrial regions were by definition not self-sufficient. Industrial Lancashire and Cheshire, whose output was more varied than some other regions, nonetheless had to import, from other British regions or foreign countries, food, intermediate industrial products, consumer goods of all kinds, and, of course, raw cotton. It exported cotton textiles and, increasingly, engineering products. Important though the backward linkages to coal, chemicals and iron were within Lancashire, they were overshadowed by its need to export the great bulk of its prime speciality, textiles. The question then is, to what degree did Lancashire and other industrial regions owe their ability to export outside their own borders to their existence within a wider national polity? It is unanswerable in any precise way, because we cannot know what alternative political entity would have existed if Great Britain had not been a unitary state. But one can quickly indicate the limits facing any one region assuming that it was politically independent. There would not necessarily have been a British market, nor can the existence of more than a fraction of the existing foreign markets which Britain enjoyed in the real world be assumed. Britain's export success in the eighteenth century depended partly on cost advantage, but also on its ability to exclude foreigners, particularly from the important North American market. This ability depended on naval strength which was in part a function of the ability to pay, which depended in turn on national size.

As well as the all-important aspect of market size, the national polity offered other important benefits such as the patent system, a stable political system and a predictable legal one. There were aspects of economic development which were inseparable from particular regions, apart from coal. Regions generated much, although not all, of their labour supply and much of their own capital – although their ability to produce capital was ultimately linked with their level of economic activity which, again, cannot be divorced from national developments. In general, attempts to elevate the importance of regions in the British Industrial Revolution rest on an incorrect analogy with European industrialisation; since that started by borrowing British technology, the issue of market size and its relationship to inventive activity did not arise.

It is less apposite to criticise those who emphasise the importance of London, since theirs is not an argument about industrialisation *per se*. However, it is worth noting that, just as industrial regions could not have flourished without the market provided by the rest of Great Britain, so London would not necessarily have flourished between 1750 and 1850 and later without industrialisation elsewhere in the British Isles. Proponents of London's autonomy point to the continuation of a distinctive London economy, based on overseas commerce, services and consumer industries, over the whole period. But the fact that it continued does not prove that it would have done so in different circumstances, and here a brief comparison with Antwerp is instructive. The commercial hub of northern and western Europe in the early sixteenth century, Antwerp suffered a sharp decline as its hinterland experienced civil war and political and religious division. In the same way, London depended in part on prosperity and stability in other parts of Britain. A prosperous hinterland enlarged the tax revenues, land rents and returns on capital which flowed into the metropolis, as well as providing a market for London goods and services. Without industrialisation, Britain would have faced a bleak future as an increasingly overpopulated island and London's income would have been correspondingly diminished. London also depended in part on the prosperity of Britain's overseas commerce; not only did the effective defence of this depend on the size of the national polity, but during the Napoleonic Wars the ability to find the huge sums of foreign currency needed to fight, and to maintain foreign allies, owed itself largely to the tremendous advantages Britain now enjoyed in world textile markets. Even during peacetime, overseas commerce depended increasingly on Britain's ability to absorb imports and produce the exports to pay from them – both largely functions of industrialisation. Finally, industrialisation elsewhere cut costs for London's own industries and consumers, by supplying cheaper coal, iron, clothing, glass, pottery and other essentials.

Table

Table 6.1 Coal production

	million tons (tonnes)
1750	6.2 (6.3)
1775	8.8 (9.0)
1800	15.0 (15.3)
1830	30.9 (31.5)
1845–9 (annual average)	55.9 (57.0)

After B.R. Mitchell, *British Historical Statistics* (Cambridge, 1988)

Further reading

R. Szostak, *The Role of Transportation in the Industrial Revolution: a comparison of Britain and France* (Montreal and Kingston, 1991) is an important overview; E. Pawson, *The Turnpike Roads of Eighteenth-century Britain* (1977) highlights the significance of turnpiking as an innovation; J.E. Shepherd and G.M. Walton, *Shipping, Maritime Trade and the Economic Development of Colonial North America* (Cambridge, 1972) lucidly sets out the result (in their case for colonial producers) of a shift in demand curves as a result of transport change. Hyde, *British Iron Industry* (see Chapter 5) and T.S. Ashton, *An Eighteenth-century Industrialist: Peter Stubs of Warrington 1756–1806* (Manchester, 1939) also testify to the impact of transport change. D. Gerhold, 'Productivity change in road transport before and after turnpiking, 1690–1840', *EcHR*, 49 (1996) pp. 491–515 and S. Ville, 'Total factor productivity in the English shipping industry: the North-East coal trade 1700–1850', *EcHR*, 39 (1986), pp. 240–61 are invaluable for their respective subjects. There is also a debate following the latter between W.J. Hausman and Ville in *ibid.*, 40 (1987), pp. 588–97 and J. Armstrong and Hausman in *ibid.*, 46 (1993), pp. 607–12, but all protagonists agree that real costs did decline. For canals see G. Turnbull, 'Canals, coal and regional growth during the industrial revolution' *EcHR*, 40 (1987), pp. 537–60. For regions see S. Pollard, *Peaceful Conquest: The Industrialisation of Europe 1760–1970* (Oxford, 1981); his views gain some support from J. Langton, 'The industrial revolution and the regional geography of England', *Transactions of the Institute of British Geographers*, 9 (1984), pp. 145–67, but see the more sceptical view of D. Gregory, 'The production of regions in England's industrial revolution', *Journal of Historical Geography*, 14 (1988), pp. 50–8. P. Hudson, *Regions and Industries: A Perspective on the Industrial Revolution in Britain* (Cambridge, 1989) contains case-studies. For London-centred accounts see C.H. Lee (see Introduction) and the enjoyably knockabout performance in W.D. Rubinstein, *Capitalism, Culture and Decline in Britain 1750–1990* (1993), which suggests (p. 44) that historians' obsession with manufacturing industry may have an 'underlying sexual undertone'. An emphasis on the centrality of London and southern England is also found in P.J. Cain and A.G. Hopkins, *British Imperialism: Innovation and Expansion 1688–1914* (1993); J.R. Ward's 'The industrial revolution and British imperialism, 1750–1850', *EcHR*, 47 (1994), pp. 44–65 is a valuable antidote.

B.W. E. Alford, *W.D.& H.O. Wills and the Development of the U.K. Tobacco Industry 1786–1965* (1973).

R. Davis, *The Rise of the English Shipping Industry in the Seventeenth and Eighteenth Centuries* (Newton Abbot, 1962).

J.L. de Mann, *The Cloth Industry in the West of England from 1640 to 1880* (Oxford, 1971).

D.F. Harrison, 'Bridges and economic development, 1300–1800', *EcHR*, 45 (1992), pp. 240–61.

H. Leibenstein, 'Allocative efficiency and X-efficiency', *American Economic Review*, 56 (1966), pp. 392–415; it is excerpted in L. Putterman, *The Economic Nature of the Firm* (Cambridge, 1986).

A.E. Musson, *The Growth of British Industry* (1978).

D.J. Rowe, *The Economy of the North-East in the Nineteenth Century* (Stanley, 1973).

L.D. Schwarz, *London in the Age of Industrialisation* (Cambridge, 1992).

S. Ville, 'The growth of specialisation in English shipowning 1750–1850', *EcHR*, 46 (1993), pp. 702–22.

Chapter 7

Industrialisation and living standards

From the 1840s or earlier, contemporary commentators had drawn attention to the deleterious effects of industrialisation, such as the ill-health and poor housing endured by many workers. This theme was taken up by historians and became a long-running debate between two schools of thought: one, characterised as the pessimistic, consisting of those who agreed with the contemporary analysis and thought that industrialisation was negative, or only weakly positive, for living standards; the other, the optimistic, consisting of those who thought the opposite.

The origin of many pessimistic views lay with Marx, who believed that workers were not paid the full value of their labour. He blamed this on the extraction of profit, or in his terminology surplus value, by capitalists. Since he believed that it was labour, rather than capital, which produced the surplus, it followed that workers were cheated of their due. Non-Marxian economics, of course, sees profit as the return to capital, which is a factor of production, for its contribution to output. Marx did not actually say that workers would be worse off under capitalism, although he often implied it, but he believed that capitalism worked in part by cheapening labour power, or in other words reducing the value of human capital, through the subdivision of labour, a view discussed in Chapter 3. So far as this converted skilled workers into unskilled workers, it would reduce wages and therefore 'immiserate' – another Marxian word – the workforce; furthermore work itself would become more and more tedious and hateful.

Marx did not influence all those historians who were pessimistic about the effects of the Industrial Revolution. Much British historiography has been influenced by the works of J.L. and Barbara

Hammond, whose early twentieth-century brand of progressive liberalism influenced their negative views of the Industrial Revolution period. In contrast, another non-Marxist pessimist was Arthur Bryant, a purveyor of nostalgia whose volumes on English history still fill the shelves of second-hand bookshops and older middle-class households. His condemnation of industrialisation stemmed from a yearning for an imagined rural past and a dislike of capitalism which had quasi-fascist origins. But Marx's views have probably exerted some influence on most academic pessimists even if they have not themselves been Marxist.

Optimists grounded their arguments on the figures for growth. Their model was a straightforward one in which increases in national income per person inevitably fed through into living standards. Some modified optimists, or more neutral scholars, have pointed to possibilities which would have reduced the gains for some – perhaps many – of the population. These possibilities include an increase in inequality; differential regional wage trends so that gains were not equally spread; and problems of urban growth which reduced the gains in welfare that would have accrued from higher incomes.

Any model suffers from the problem that a number of causal factors were working together to affect living standards during the Industrial Revolution and it is probably impossible to accurately disentangle their different impacts. Marx's critique was of the workings of capitalism, rather than of industrialisation *per se*. Other influences such as agricultural change, population growth, war and urbanisation, as well as industrialisation, must have had some effect. More intelligent historians recognise the complexity of these different influences and temper their opinions accordingly.

Real wages and other evidence

Until recent years one of the greatest problems in the optimist-pessimist debate was the paucity of real-wage data; furthermore it was difficult to square that which did exist with the data for real incomes per person, which was generated independently. The relation of the two is discussed in the Appendix, but broadly speaking they should change at approximately the same rate. The income estimates for the Industrial Revolution period which were available before the mid-1980s, notably those of Deane and Cole, suggested

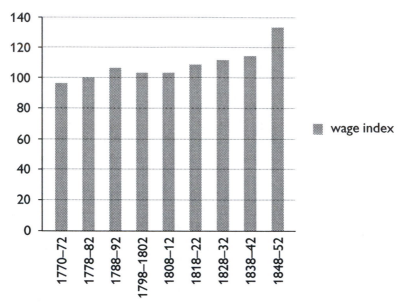

Figure 7.1 Real wages (after Table 7.1)

a considerable increase. Estimates for real wages varied depending on the geographical area to which they related, the dates from and to which they were compiled, the cost-of-living indices which the compiler used, and other factors. Some estimates suggested rapid growth others suggested that growth was much slower than the Deane and Cole income estimates. From the mid-1980s estimates of income per person and real wages started to converge. Crafts' and Harley's revised national income figures suggested much lower growth in income per person than Deane's and Cole's. And recent recalculations of real wages by Charles Feinstein, more thorough and complete than any before, have produced figures which are reasonably close to the Crafts-Harley estimates of national income per person. The two sets of figures are discussed in the Appendix; their similarity is, in itself, grounds for viewing them with greater confidence than could be attached to earlier estimates. For the purposes of this discussion Feinstein's wage figures will be taken as the best which are available.

Feinstein's figures show that the pessimists were broadly correct about the level of real wages. Wages grew slowly; for long periods they either did not grow at all or actually fell back, while severe recessions could also reduce real wages substantially. The figures in Table 7.1 do not show regional and occupational variations, although these are incorporated within the overall total, as are women's earnings. Regional variations have been mentioned in previous chapters. Real wages throughout the north of England and much of the Midlands grew rapidly throughout the second half of the eighteenth century. Conversely, real wages in London and the rest of the south started to fall from around 1750 onwards. The majority of London wage-earners, relatively well-paid, could experience some decline without being reduced to dire poverty. If Voth's argument, discussed in Chapter 4, is correct they may have partly made up for the decline in hourly wages by working longer hours. The full force of the wage decline was experienced by the rural workers of southern England, whose standard of living had never been more than extremely modest. From the 1780s onwards their real wages fluctuated, more often falling by as much as 10 per cent below the low level of that decade than rising above it. In 1850 their wages were still no higher than they had been seventy years earlier.

Changes in the relative wage levels of broad occupational groupings were not so marked as regional variations over the period 1770–1850. Agricultural wages had always been low; they grew more slowly than average, but not by much, because the rapid rise of northern agricultural wages counteracted the dismal experience of the south. The most rapid growth, but again not by a large margin, was in transport and building wages. Wages in mining and manufacturing grew by slightly more than the average.

What the national figures do not allow for is the effect on family earnings of changes in the participation rates of different groups, such as women and children. A study of this has been made by Sarah Horrell and Jane Humphries. Their methodology is different from Feinstein's as their earnings figures were compiled from over 1,000 family budgets collected from the 1790s to the 1860s. So their figures act as a further check on his, although they are almost certainly less reliable because, while their total sample is large, the number of budgets is often quite small when broken down by period and occupational grouping. Applying Feinstein's cost-of-living index to their figures indicates that the real-wage increase they find for adult men is not too different from Feinstein's. Additionally, their figures suggest that by the end of their period the increase in family earnings was around 10 per cent less than the increase in male earnings, because of declining female and child participation, although the discrepancy is much less – or the other way – earlier in the period.

In recent years a new source of evidence on living standards has become available to historians; this is data on changes in height. Initially this was touted as a wonderful means of skirting the apparently impassable bog of disagreement in which the debate about real wages had become mired. Unfortunately, height estimates were quickly subject to technical debates over statistical issues which rendered their conclusions uncertain. Subsequently, as shown above, the real-wage issue has come much closer to resolution. Height measurements can therefore be placed where they probably belong, as extremely interesting adjuncts to measurements of real wages and other indicators such as mortality, but not a complete panacea for the optimist-pessimist debate.

Adult height is regarded by physiologists as an excellent indicator of 'nutritional status' in childhood and adolescence. This potentially misleading term is not a measure of the input of food, but an output measure: it refers to the interaction between diet, health and other environmental factors which might affect growth. As such, it has been argued that it captures the realities of living standards better than do real wages, which reflect command over priced goods and services but not over vital unpriced ones such as air and water quality. Height measures childhood and adolescent experience but, if it is assumed that children experience roughly the same living standards as their parents, then their adult height will be a retrospective measure of living standards when they were children.

Since heights in the past were not recorded for a random sample of the population but for selected groups such as military recruits, the datasets are potentially subject to changes in extraneous influences such as recruitment policy or the relative attractions of army life. This can lead to statistical aberrations and necessitates complex and problematical ways of overcoming these. A dataset of recruits which showed some gain in average heights from c. 1790–1820 and a decline thereafter has been challenged on these grounds.

Other studies suggest that decline was under way from 1790 and continued throughout the whole period to the 1850s. So there is disagreement over details but broad agreement over the broad fact of long-term decline, as opposed to the long-term rise one might expect from the real-wage increase.

As well as disagreements about statistical techniques, there are methodological problems about the use of height as an indicator of nutritional status. Essentially they revolve around how widely the latter term is drawn. Thus it has been suggested that, if there was some rise in heights in the early nineteenth century, one reason for this was a sharp reduction in the incidence of smallpox. This could be seen as an improvement in the disease environment and therefore in nutritional status, on the widest possible interpretation of that term. Or it could be seen as a one-off change that could not really be counted as an improvement in the standard of living, although it was undoubtedly very important for those who would have otherwise caught the disease.

The problem of sunlight deprivation is even more awkward. A severe lack of sunlight can cause rickets, that is a failure of the bones to calcify properly during growth. According to medical textbooks, this can affect height, and Peter Kirby has suggested that it might have affected the height of miners, since boys went down the mines at a young age. But miners earned quite good wages, so should we view their lack of height as directly correlated with poor nutritional status in childhood, even though in other respects young miners, unpleasant as their working conditions were, were probably better off than many other children? Mild rickets did not stop people leading a normal and active life, but it may have made them shorter.

Kirby's insight could be extended, although as far as the author is aware it has not been, to height evidence in general. Early twentieth-century doctors believed that rickets was endemic in the British urban population. Modern medical science would attribute this largely to the pall of smoke which lay over large towns due to the ubiquitous use of coal, exacerbated by narrow streets which further blocked out sunlight. If rickets had a significant effect on height, this might partially resolve a number of the puzzles which currently attach to all height evidence. One of these is, as noted, the apparent tendency for height to decline until the mid-nineteenth century in spite of the modest rise in real wages. Another is that, although the heights of rural dwellers seem to have declined in line with other heights, there was a persistent tendency for rural dwellers to be taller in spite of the very low level of rural wages. A final and particularly inexplicable point is the very slow growth in working-class height in the second half of the nineteenth century, in spite of major gains in real wages, an improvement in the disease environment and a reduction in child labour. Attribution of rickets as a factor in height would help to explain all these puzzles. As time went by more and more people would live in an almost permanently smoky environment because coal consumption was increasing rapidly, and towns grew into conurbations from which smoke did not disperse easily.

Finally, there is the paradoxical fact that, according to budget evidence and in spite of their lower incomes, the rural poor actually had a superior diet in terms of its nutritional composition than did the urban poor, thus affording another possible explanation for the disparity between rural and urban heights. There may have been a number of reasons for this apparent paradox, including the relative expense of coal in the countryside – so country dwellers ate more to make up for lack of heat; the simple fact that agricultural workers spent more energy on work that the average urban worker would have done; and the use by urban dwellers of larger quantities of expensive, if tastier, food and drink products such as fish, tea and alcohol. This highlights the fact that taste influences the choice of diet and does not always yield the most efficient result. Consequently, while there can be no doubt that there is a correlation between height and living standards, broadly conceived, the two may coincide less neatly than some historians think. Nevertheless the height evidence concurs with the real-wage evidence in painting a depressing picture of living standards from the late eighteenth to the mid-nineteenth centuries. If height actually fell, and leaving aside the possibility of rickets as a factor, it suggests that urban areas had many disamenities which tended to counteract the higher wages earned by their inhabitants.

Apart from height, there are other indicators of urban disamenities, or more bluntly of urban squalor and deprivation. In an important article Simon Szreter and Graham Mooney suggest that mortality in many large English and Scottish urban areas rose sharply between the 1820s and the 1830s before levelling off; it fell again around 1850 but remained at a dismally high level, actually above that of the 1820s, until as late as 1870 or so. The likely explanation for this starts with the continuing rapid population growth in towns and cities. At some point local government, geared to a small-scale world of market towns or rural parishes, more or less collapsed. As a result, overcrowded housing and lack of water and sewage facilities, problems which were not new but which got worse as urban areas expanded, became more lethal because the breakdown of government restricted the taking of ameliorative measures. The mortality of infants and small children seems to have risen particularly sharply, these being the groups who were most liable to intestinal infections and other diseases transmitted in overcrowded areas lacking clean water. Smallpox also returned, as local government, which had hitherto arranged for mass vaccination of the poor, failed to carry this out. These conjectures are supported by the fact that southern cities, which expanded more slowly, had lower mortality than northern ones in spite of lower real wages. From the 1830s on legislation enabled improvements in urban government to be made but conservatism, parsimony and the continued increase in population meant that necessary changes came about very slowly.

This suggestion helps to explain the lack of correlation between height data and wage data, since the latter would not take into account the problems of living in rapidly expanding cities which are captured by the measurement of height. There are, however, still substantial anomalies between the different sets of data and a lot of work needs to be done to resolve them, although the non-availability of data may prevent complete resolution. The most important anomaly is that the average mortality experience for Britain seems to have remained roughly the same throughout the whole period from 1800 to the 1860s, suggesting that outside the large urban areas there was a reduction in mortality. This conclusion arises because the inhabitants of large urban areas formed an increasing proportion of the population, and had much higher mortality than average; if mortality elsewhere had not declined, then the national total would actually have increased through the simple arithmetical fact that more people lived in high mortality areas. However, an improvement in mortality elsewhere, whilst consistent with real-wage evidence, does not tie up with the height evidence, which suggests general decline. One partial resolution of this problem is that the height evidence almost all refers to predominantly working-class groups, namely military recruits and convicts. If working-class experience was considerably worse than the average, then this helps to explain the lack of correlation between height and mortality data.

The fact that real wages seem to have increased at a slower rate than national income per person does suggest that working-class income increased at a lower rate than the average, or in other words, that there was an increase in inequality between the skilled, including the middle classes, and the unskilled. A few years ago Jeffrey Williamson suggested on theoretical grounds that this might occur in the early stages of industrialisation, and believed that he had found evidence for this. Both his theory and his evidence have been criticised. In particular, his evidence for a more rapid rise in middle-class income rests on a minuscule sample which cannot be given credence. However, the question can be approached from another direction. The real incomes of the upper and middle classes may have diverged because of differential price changes in the goods which were bought by different groups.

Price indices used in measuring real wages are constructed by taking a representative 'basket' of goods in which the weightings correspond to the average spending on such goods. Feinstein's real-wage series uses a price index which accords weightings of approximately 65 per cent for food, 10 per cent each for rent and drink, a bit less for clothing and the small amount remaining for fuel and light. (The actual weights for each item change slightly over time.) The index is incomplete because it leaves out such items as cooking and eating utensils and transport services, all of which even working-class consumers would buy if only on a small scale. However, it is based on extensive budget evidence and is no doubt broadly correct. Because of the high proportion of spending on food, its high cost throughout the period was a heavy burden on the working-class consumer. Relative food prices were on a rising trend throughout the late eighteenth century, and rose particularly sharply during the Napoleonic Wars as the European grain trade was disrupted. After the wars they fell back somewhat but remained relatively high due to the Corn Laws, only repealed in 1846, and to rapid European population growth which meant that food supply barely kept pace with demand.

Working-class living standards, therefore, were held back by adverse trends in food prices, exacerbated by rents which rose at a much more rapid rate than other prices from around 1830 onwards. Middle- and upper-class living standards would have exhibited very different tendencies because food was a much smaller part of the middle-class budget. Instead, manufactures in the form of utensils, furnishings, ornaments, books and newspapers formed a significant proportion of spending, as did transport services. Thus the improvements in manufacturing and transport productivity would have benefited this group far more than they did the working class.

It seems likely, therefore, that there was a growth in inequality over most if not all of the Industrial Revolution period, caused by differential price changes. Only after 1860 or so was this reversed as food prices started to fall relative to other prices. The probability of a more rapid growth in middle- and upper-class living standards helps to explain the faster rise in average income per person than in real wages. In addition, the real-wage figures may well understate the improvement for better-paid workers, such as miners and most skilled workers, whose families would have spent a higher proportion of their incomes on manufactures than is allowed for by Feinstein. In reality there was not a sharp gap in income between working class and middle class, but a continuum between the better-off members of the former and the poorer members of the latter.

Finally, it is important to realise that upper- and middle-class gains did not go entirely to increasing their consumption, but partly to higher saving. This was particularly the case during the wars, but the increase in the savings ratio also financed the long-term rise in the investment ratio, from around 6 per cent in the mid-eighteenth century to around 11 per cent by the mid-nineteenth.

Explaining living standards

If an historical debate is a competition, then in the standard-of-living debate the pessimists are the winners. This is a conclusion which would not have surprised Karl Marx; but orthodox economic theory can explain it as well as or better than Marxian economics. At the root of the slow and erratic growth in real wages, and the even more dismal experience recorded in the height and mortality data, were two basic phenomena, which were exacerbated by various ancillary effects.

The first phenomenon, discussed in the Appendix, was that, dramatic though change was in some sectors of industry, the average growth in industrial productivity was slow. If, as seems possible, agricultural productivity growth was relatively slow during this period as well, that constituted a further brake on total growth. The result of this was a slow growth in income per person: this in itself was fundamental. However favourable or unfavourable other influences, average living standards could not have risen rapidly, because technical change and other forces for productivity improvement were unevenly applied throughout the economy, many sectors remaining almost unchanged for long periods.

The effects of uneven technical change were exacerbated by the effects of the second phenomenon, the rapid growth of population. The pressures of diminishing returns constantly reduced the potential gains from innovation and capital investment. These views were put forward at the time, in a schematic way, by the economist Thomas Malthus, and elaborated by his followers. (Hence pre-industrial population growth is commonly referred to as a 'Malthusian trap'.) With hindsight, we can see that technical change was ultimately to overcome diminishing returns, but it was not so obvious at the time. It is true that if the wage experience of the north, where innovation was most effectively applied, had been universal, national real-wage gains would have been substantial, but the effect of diminishing returns was strong enough to ensure virtually no gains in hourly real-wage rates in London and the rest of the south over the whole period 1750–1850. There was, no doubt, some technical and organisational change in London industries and southern agriculture so that output per person per hour rose, but this was counterbalanced by declining female and child participation and by increasing underemployment and casualisation among the male workforce. Rising population was not just a southern problem; for a considerable period, perhaps up to the second decade of the nineteenth century, it had neutral or positive implications for the north and Midlands: industry was easily able to absorb the growth and urban areas were not yet uncontrollably large and crowded. From then on, however, the growth of population, to which was added migration from Ireland, posed economic problems in the north too; these were not so much a result of lack of employment but, as noted earlier, of the problems caused by gross overcrowding in urban areas.

If population growth had been caused by industrialisation, its role in diminishing living standards would be viewed differently because it would not have been an independent force. But as Chapter 4 showed, it is unlikely that there was a transmission mechanism from industrialisation to population growth until well into the nineteenth century; and even then it is uncertain whether industrialisation was an accelerator or a retardant. On the other hand, if population growth had been a significant cause of industrialisation, then again one would perceive it differently. The benefits brought by industrialisation would have offset the problems posed by population growth and the latter could hardly be singled out as a villain. However, there is no reason to suppose that population growth had a significant causal role in industrialisation. A reasonably sized population was necessary to ensure an adequate market size, but this was in place in the mid-eighteenth century and from then on, as suggested in Chapter 4, population growth was not a significant causal factor.

Population growth was not confined to Britain. Between 1815 and 1850, the combined population of France, Germany and Italy grew from 71 million to 93 million. Population elsewhere in Europe increased at a similar rate or faster, putting an immense strain on European food supplies. Britain, with its own increasing population, found it increasingly difficult to feed itself, and in the 1840s had to import large quantities of European grain at a time when European prices had risen sharply. So British food prices, having been propped up for twenty years by the Corn Laws, remained high even when these were repealed.

The price of food imports bore particular weight because the price of Britain's main export, cotton textiles, fell rapidly due to productivity increases. This meant that Britain's terms of trade, discussed in Chapter 4, deteriorated rapidly in the first half of the nineteenth century. The implications of this need exploration: suppose productivity in cotton textiles had risen, and the price fallen, more slowly than was actually the case; sales abroad would have been smaller because of the higher prices, but they might not have fallen much because Britain's competitive advantage was so great that British textiles undercut Continental goods by a large margin. In other words, the price elasticity of demand was likely to be quite low; only if prices had been much higher than they were would Britain have become uncompetitive. So on the assumption of a limited rise in prices, Britain's revenue from cotton textile exports might actually have been larger, thus enabling a larger quantity of Continental imports to be purchased. This seems like an argument against technical change, but the full implications have not been spelt out. Britain would have had to devote more resources to making each unit of textiles exported since, if revenue from exports had actually risen, the total of resources – capital and labour – devoted to exports would have had to have grown. So against the gain in the power to import, there would have been a reduction in home production of other commodities. In addition, home consumers would have had to pay more for their textiles. The deterioration in the terms of trade is, therefore, something of a red herring in the search for explanations of lower living standards. Its effect must have been limited. The big problem was food prices and not until those fell sharply would the working-class consumer really benefit from industrialisation.

This fall did not start until the 1860s; it was a late, but probably the single most important, fruit of industrialisation. Until then, British and European agricultural productivity had been growing but could do little more than keep pace with population. Industrialisation accelerated improvement through the use of artificial fertilisers, improved implements and – although this mainly occurred later – the introduction of machinery. Transport improvements within Europe cut the cost of distribution and, most important, the opening-up of North America and other great temperate areas to large-scale food production through the medium of railways, and the reduction of intercontinental transport costs through the development of iron ships, brought about a massive reduction in the relative and absolute price of food.

One of the ancillary effects which exacerbated the problems facing the poor was the Revolutionary and Napoleonic Wars (the wars), which began in 1792. The wars' possible effects on the wider economy were discussed in Chapter 4. Since they occurred when the supply/demand of European foodstuffs was already finely balanced, due to population increase, they caused a sharp increase in food prices; but at the time this was less of a problem than it might have been, because the high level of government expenditure led to plentiful employment opportunities. Once they were over, food prices remained high because of population pressure and the Corn Laws, and there was a shorter period of intermittently depressed economic activity while government spending and the circulation of money were restricted in order to return to gold backing for the currency, achieved in 1821. The wars also left Britain with an enormous National Debt, much of which had been taken on at the inflated prices of the war years. Interest on this had to be paid. Except for the small proportion held by foreigners, the interest flowed to British citizens and so its purchasing power was not lost to the economy. However, the money to pay the interest had to come from taxation, which fell on many items of common consumption, such as tea, sugar and beer, as well as items whose price entered into living standards indirectly, such as bricks. The National Debt was predominantly held by members of the upper and middle classes, who were the only groups who could afford to subscribe to it. So the interest on it was a direct transfer from consumers, who included the working classes, to a select group of the better-off. Gareth Stedman-Jones and others have highlighted the extent to which the Chartists, and other political and social protest groups, were not anti-capitalist but rather opponents of the burdens of taxation and debt. 'Fundholder' was a common term of opprobrium used by William Cobbett and other radicals. Their target was a real one: interest on debt was around 10 per cent of national income in 1820, and other government expenditure doubled that, so taxation took around 20 per cent of national income. By 1850 debt service had fallen slightly and other government expenditure remained about the same, but national income had doubled, and so by that time taxation took only 10 per cent of national income and its incidence was not a real problem. However, until the early 1840s it had had a real impact on the living standards of working people, whilst giving them few benefits.

Another source of income transfer from the poor to a select group of the better-off was rent. Contemporary economists such as David Ricardo paid rent a great deal of attention, following Malthus in their fear that rising population with static supplies of land would push up food prices and hence agricultural rents. In the long run land was not fixed in quantity, due to the 'ghost acreage' of the New World and the technical advances which allowed it to supply Europe with food. In the short and medium term, food prices did rise but since agricultural rent was subsumed in these it does not need a separate discussion. However, urban rent was also susceptible to population pressure and was paid directly by the consumer. Few people owned the houses in which they lived and therefore the returns from increasing urban rent and land prices went to the original landholder, or to speculators who had bought urban land, or to houseowners. These last were a variegated bunch and, although some of them may have started poor, most were members of the middle class who chose to invest their savings in bricks and mortar.

According to Feinstein, working-class house rent doubled between 1770 and 1850, compared with an average increase of around 30 per cent in all prices and an increase of around 80 per cent in money earnings. Relative to other prices, rent only started to increase some time after the Napoleonic Wars. This is what we would expect, given that, in the early stages of growth, housing could easily be built on nearby agricultural land but still be reasonably close to town centres. But as urban areas grew ever larger this became impossible and, since public transport was far too expensive for the working classes, they had to find housing in already crowded central areas and inner suburbs. To add to the pressures, workplaces themselves took an increasing proportion of land as work moved out of the home and into factories, while from the 1830s railways were another consumer of land. All this increased the demands on urban land and thus on rent levels, and since efficiency gains in house construction were limited, there was no favourable influence to counteract rent rises. Given the weighting of rent in working-class budgets, its increase relative to the general price level can be reckoned to have reduced working-class real incomes by, very approximately, 5 per cent. Practically all of this occurred in the short period 1830–50, so the increase in rent partially counterbalanced the simultaneous reduction in the burden of taxation. As with taxation, which transferred income from a wide spectrum of the population to a small group of better-off fundholders, rent was a transfer from the majority of people who were tenants to one small, and arbitrarily selected, group of land- and house-owners.

The increase in rent can be viewed in two ways: as the market working – crudely, unfairly, but effectively – to price land at the level which people were prepared to pay; or, because it was so crude and unfair, as an example of markets not working effectively – of market failure. If it was the latter, then an even more serious failure was caused by urban expansion and by the slowness of local government in Britain to adjust to it. Public health was a good which needed effective authority to ensure it was not damaged. Some of its components were priceable: water supply and sewage disposal could both be paid for on a per-house basis through the familiar mechanism of house rates. Others, such as clean streets, could only be financed by a collective levy. But whether priceable or not, public health services needed authorities with mandatory powers, for instance to lay water and sewage pipes. It also helped to have consumers who were willing to pay, and many were not; in the past these things had usually been free, and most people did not understand the direct connection between, say, clean water and their child's health; so there was information failure as well as market failure. The failure to provide effective local government until it was too late is one of the chief indictments against the ruling political groups of this period. But, as so often, blame is difficult to attribute precisely. Whereas the Corn Laws were an act of naked selfishness, the failure of urban government crept up unawares as population and urbanisation continued their inexorable growth. And when remediable action did begin, it was not so much Parliament that hampered rapid improvement but rather the middling groups at a local level – the 'shopocracy' – as well as consumers of all classes. Estimates have been made of the 'cost' of these urban disamenities to the average worker by Jeffrey Williamson, but in the end they cannot get us very far because shorter life spans, for example, cannot be costed in any meaningful way. One can agree with Williamson that, in the north where urban mortality was worse, the urban–rural wage differential seems much less favourable for urban workers and their families in the light of disamenities. In southern towns and cities wage levels were lower but so were both rural wages and urban disamenities, so the equation is rather different. And London offered such a large wage premium that, in spite of disamenities, it must have offered the rural migrant substantial gains. Paradoxically, the biggest gainers from real wage increases, when a notional cost for urban disamenities is subtracted, were northern and Midlands agricultural workers, joined later in the period by their Scottish brethren as Scottish industrialisation got under way and raised both urban and rural wages.

Finally, and as another example of political selfishness, there was the fate of the Poor Law. The English Poor Law, dating from the sixteenth century, was a remarkably comprehensive – for the period – system by which a minimum living standard was assured to those deemed unable to support themselves, such as the old and orphans. By the late eighteenth century it was coming under strain as poor rural agricultural labourers and their families were increasingly included in its coverage, and around 2 per cent of national income was devoted to it. Further pressure on expenditure in the aftermath of the Napoleonic Wars led to an attempt to sharply limit coverage in the New Poor Law of 1834. While this never fully realised its aim of giving relief only to those willing to be incarcerated in workhouses, it did cut down on Poor Law expenditure.

Marx thought capitalism was to blame for the miseries, as he saw them, of the Industrial Revolution. Unless one accepts Marx's peculiar economic theories, capitalism was part of the solution to the underlying problem of diminishing returns, although it did pose problems of its own. If capitalism is defined as private property plus free markets, then it was probably the most effective means of stimulating agricultural and industrial improvement. The institution of private property guaranteed the security of profit, which stimulated invention and innovation; the existence of profit also ensured that capital was allocated to projects on which it would earn the best return. Broadly speaking, these were likely to be projects which were best for the economy. Free markets provided the other half of the equation – the ability to sell goods on which a profit could be made. They also ensured that the profits from innovation did not in the long term flow to the innovators but were competed away, thus leading to falling real prices.

But not all was rosy with capitalism. First, the distribution of private property started off as highly unequal, and the subsequent accumulation of capital and increase in rent may have added to that inequality. Second, free markets can produce detrimental results when goods are unpriced or where public action is required to ensure their effective distribution, as with water supplies; here the market can fail. So the problems of capitalism were inequality and market failure in specific circumstances, not private property or the existence of markets *per se*.

Although few would accept Marxian economics, the tendency to accept Marx's pessimism about living standards – which to a considerable degree was justified – has led in the popular mind, and among many historians, to a transposition of the causes of poor living standards. Since a villain there must be, industrialisation rather than capitalism has become cast in that role. Yet industrialisation was even less to blame than capitalism; with the aid of the market mechanisms of capitalism, industrialisation created jobs, and most of those jobs paid better wages than those available before. However, industry and modern services such as transport were less than half of the economy for the Industrial Revolution period, and even in that half productivity grew slowly, so much of the wage gain conferred by industrialisation was swallowed up by higher food prices. Added to this were the burdens caused by taxation to pay interest on the National Debt, mainly a product of eighteenth- and early nineteenth-century wars, and the increase in urban rent. Industrialisation was, of course, closely implicated in the latter because it was associated with urbanisation. Although many urban jobs were in services rather than manufacturing, they existed because manufacturing increasingly clustered in towns, in order to reap economies of scale and to benefit from cheap coal. The heavy dependence of British industrialisation on coal added to the pollution problems of large urban areas, so industrialisation bore some responsibility for the specific problems posed by urbanisation, although to a greater extent these were caused by market failure. Finally, industrialisation created jobs, such as those in mines and textile mills, which were often unhealthy and unsafe. Arguments based on health issues cannot be pushed too far, however, because many old-established workshop trades were deleterious to health as well. And if there was a period when women and children were exploited because of industrialisation, it lasted only a short time before economic forces tended to reduce women's and children's paid work.

It is irrational to blame industrialisation for most of the social problems of the late eighteenth to mid-nineteenth centuries. The worst enemy was not growth, but lack of growth in the face of rising population. The Prussian peasant, the Viennese craftworker and the Parisian labourer, all in countries where industrialisation was only beginning in 1850, were far worse off during the period of Britain's Industrial Revolution than the British factory hand. It was industrialisation, first in Britain and then elsewhere, which provided the main escape route from the Malthusian trap.

Table

Table 7.1 Real wages

	Index
1770–72	96
1778–82	100
1788–92	106
1798–1802	103
1808–12	103
1818–22	108
1828–32	111
1838–42	114
1848–52	133

After Feinstein, 'Pessimism perpetuated', Table 5, Column 2 (see further reading); figures are for wage-earners' real weekly earnings, adjusted for unemployment

Further reading

C.H. Feinstein, 'Pessimism perpetuated: real wages and the standard of living in Britain during and after the industrial revolution', *JEH*, 58 (1998), pp. 625–58 seems likely to replace all earlier estimates of national wage changes. S. Horrell and J. Humphries, 'Old questions, new data and alternative perspectives: families' living standards in the industrial revolution', *JEH*, 52 (1992), pp. 849–80 for family incomes. For regional variations E.H. Hunt, 'Industrialisation and regional inequality' (see Chapter 3) and L.D. Schwarz, 'The standard of living in the long run: London, 1700–1860', *EcHR*, 38 (1985), pp. 24–41, summarised in Schwarz, *London* (see Chapter 6). For inequality Feinstein's 'The rise and fall of the Williamson curve', *JEH*, 48 (1988), pp. 699–729, which is a review of J.G. Williamson, *Did British Capitalism Breed Inequality?* (Boston, 1985); Feinstein makes a strong case for stability in the relationship between different levels of money income but, as this chapter suggests, differential price changes might alter the position for real income. For mortality S. Szreter and G.

Mooney, 'Urbanisation, mortality and the standard of living debate: new estimates of the expectation of life at birth in nineteenth century British cities', *EcHR*, 51 (1998), pp. 84–112 and for urban crisis S. Szreter, 'Economic growth, disruption, deprivation, disease and death: on the importance of the politics of public health for development', *Population Development Review*, 23 (1997), pp. 693–728. For height there is a recent overview in R. Floud and B. Harris, 'Health, height and welfare: Britain 1700–1980' in R.H. Steckel and Floud, *Health and Welfare during Industrialisation* (1997); the original hypothesis based on recruits' height was put forward in R. Floud, K.W. Wachter, and A. Gregory, *Height, Health and History: Nutritional Status in the United Kingdom 1750–1980* (Cambridge, 1990). Other datasets which tend to find more consistent deterioration are discussed in: S. Nicholas and R.H. Steckel, 'Heights and living standards of English workers during the early years of industrialisation 1770–1815', *JEH*, 51 (1991), pp. 937–57; P. Johnson and Nicholas, 'Male and female living standards in England and Wales 1812–57: evidence from criminal height records', *EcHR*, 48 (1995), pp. 470–81; and Johnson and Nicholas, 'Health and welfare of women in the United Kingdom 1785–1920' in Steckel and Floud, *Health and Welfare*; see also H.J. Voth and T. Leunig, 'Did smallpox reduce height? Stature and the standard of living in London 1770–1873', *EcHR*, 49 (1996), pp. 541–60. For food consumption G. Clark, M. Huberman and P.H. Lindert, 'A British food puzzle, 1770–1850', *EcHR*, 48 (1995), pp. 215–37; and on the food price question a recent article is pessimistic on productivity increases in agriculture between 1750 and 1850: R.C. Allen, 'Tracking the agricultural revolution in England', *EcHR*, 52 (1999), pp. 209–35; see M. Overton, *Agricultural Revolution in England* (Cambridge, 1996) for an alternative view. On the roots of pessimism Arthur Bryant is discussed in Andrew Roberts, *Eminent Churchillians* (1994); J.L. and Barbara Hammond wrote a number of books, of which the most relevant is *The Town Labourer* (1917; there are more recent reprints).

S. Fairlie, 'The nineteenth-century Corn Laws reconsidered', *EcHR*, 18 (1965), pp. 562–75.

E. H. Hunt and F.W. Botham, 'Wages in Britain during the industrial revolution', *EcHR*, 40 (1987), pp. 380–99.

P. Kirby, 'Causes of short stature among coal-mining children 1823–50', *EcHR*, 48 (1995), pp. 687–99.

P.M. Solar, 'Poor relief' (see Chapter 3).

G. Stedman-Jones, 'Rethinking Chartism', in Stedman-Jones, *Languages of Class* (Cambridge, 1983).

J.G. Williamson, *Coping with City Growth* (see Chapter 3).

Chapter 8

Conclusion

Causes

A popular method of explaining the British Industrial Revolution is to list a number of factors which are thought to have contributed to it in some way. Such explanations usually include several, and sometimes all, of the following: growing demand, occurring as a result of population increase, export growth, changes in taste or some combination of these; efficient capital markets and a plentiful supply of capital; productive agriculture; a base of scientific knowledge and artisanal skills; a good transport network; Protestantism in general and Nonconformity in particular; and stable government.

This method of explanation has been aptly named the 'laundry list' approach. It is not illogical: the Industrial Revolution could simply have occurred because of the cumulative addition of a number of advantages. But neither is it very effective. In some of these areas Britain's lead over other developed economies, such as those of Holland and France, was small; in others it was non-existent or the other countries actually had an advantage. For instance, French exports may well have grown faster for most of the eighteenth century, and the Dutch had lower interest rates than Britain. So the explanation calls for a belief that a striking difference in economic development was caused by some, mainly small, advantages, which were so important that they outweighed other disadvantages. There is no particular reason assigned for this – it just was so – and this lack of explanatory rigour forms another criticism of such an explanation. It is in striking contrast to the growth models reviewed in this book, which tend to focus on one, or a very few, causal mechanisms.

Of these models of growth most fall into two camps: those which explain growth as primarily a function of capital accumulation, and those which explain it primarily as a function of innovation. In the first camp, Lewis is pre-eminent. Rostow also lays most emphasis on capital accumulation. Keynesian-type explanations, too, are essentially concerned with capital, but from a distinctive angle: the resources to construct capital assets are potentially available but are not activated due to lack of demand. Marx, followed by proto-industrialisation theorists, also sees capital accumulation as crucial. He thought innovation was a dynamic process within capitalism, but tended to focus on it as a means of cheapening labour power rather than as a motive power for investment. Finally, some thinkers such as Ashton have taken the straightforward view that savings gradually rose and, as they did so, interest rates fell and investment became more attractive.

Those who see invention and innovation as prior often fall into the orthodox neo-classical camp. Factors of production are assumed to be fully employed at the point at which industrialisation begins. Invention occurs, raising the potential return on capital, and it becomes more attractive to invest. Until recently invention was usually seen as exogenous, although some historians, notably John Harris, drew attention to the importance of learning-by-doing, while Dutton and McLeod pointed out that there were economic incentives to invention. Economists have put forward a framework in which this empirical work can be placed. The framework is provided by endogenous growth theory, which focuses on three different stimuli to invention and innovation existing within the economic system. Learning-by-doing improves organisation and techniques, but learning-by-doing will be subject to diminishing returns as there are only so many ways in which existing techniques can be improved. Macroinventions open up new scope for learning-by-doing and therefore further potential for growth. Macroinventiveness is stimulated by a minimum market size, backed up by an appropriate legal framework, which ensures that inventors reap rewards from invention. Finally, the prior existence of human capital is essential for invention, and its development contributes to the continuation of growth by increasing skills. The aspect of endogenous growth theory which focuses on the ability to earn superprofits from invention and innovation is referred to as neo-Schumpeterian as it builds on the insights of that erratic genius.

Schumpeter himself focused on the entrepreneur rather than the inventor, but in practice they were usually one and the same person, or formed a close partnership, during the Industrial Revolution period.

The evidence is against capital accumulation models. Examples such as Ashton's, based on the importance of declining interest rates, do not fit well with the evidence on the timing of investment. Furthermore the interest rates faced by businessmen changed much more slowly than national rates. The Lewis model in which low wages allowed high profits to capitalists is partially undermined because wages in industrialising areas rose rapidly, while female and child labour provided only limited opportunities for capitalists to cut wage costs. It is also clear that capital in Britain was available from a range of sources and therefore high capitalist saving was not essential, as it is in the Lewis model in which capitalists are the main source of savings. The Lewis model may have some limited validity for the period *c.* 1815–50, when population increase and Irish immigration together led to pressure on wage levels in industrial areas. But if there was an effect on the rate of investment in that period, it cannot be seen as fundamental to the Industrial Revolution: investment as a proportion of national income had already increased by around 50 per cent since 1750, and in absolute terms the increase was much greater; all this happened while Britain was fighting a series of major and expensive wars. If there was a Lewis effect on capital accumulation, it entered the stage far too late to be accorded a major role. The Lewis model might well be applicable to other episodes of rapid industrialisation, particularly those in which technology was available from outside, domestic capital was scarce and capital imports limited: Soviet Russia (where the state substituted for capitalist firms) is a case in point. But it does not hold up for Britain.

Most Keynesian-type, or demand-side, explanations also have irredeemable flaws. Population growth was too slow and changes in taste, so far as they occurred, too small, to provide sufficient incentive for investment. If war had some positive influence via government spending, it was likely to have been counterbalanced by its negative influences. The growth of exports remains as a potential source of demand growth. Almost certainly some export growth occurred as a result of falls in export prices, or of rising imports to Britain, and therefore was not autonomous. However, it is likely that there was considerable autonomous growth, particularly in the North American market. Until the 1770s or so the demand stimulus from this occurred while there was surplus labour in exporting regions; it probably absorbed so little capital that the question of whether capital was scarce or abundant is irrelevant. Export growth, therefore, probably had a positive impact on overall economic growth, but there is no easy way of linking this with invention: the impact of exports on total market size in textiles was not large until late in the century, while the genesis of the major inventions can be dated back to mid-century; in other industries where there was technical change, exports were not a major factor until much later. Autonomous export growth may well have accelerated overall growth but cannot have been an agent for decisive change.

It therefore seems that, of the two main categories of economic model, those based on invention and innovation are the more attractive. Here we are faced with the choice between exogenous and endogenous models. There is only limited evidence of close scientific links with invention, so any potential exogenous stimulus from that source is unlikely to have been important. Amateur tinkering is not a credible source of invention because significant inventions required substantial resources to develop: most inventors could not afford to view their occupation as a hobby. Exogenous theorists are then forced back to the role of chance: on this account, the random nature of inventiveness threw up a number of inventions close together, for no other reason than that random effects will sometimes produce clusters. Once the initial inventions were made, such theorists accept a role for learning-by-doing in various guises and exogenous growth, in their account, became endogenous.

However, there seems to be strong evidence that invention in Britain was not a random process. From the beginning it was driven by a combination of neo-Schumpeterian incentives, human capital endowments and learning-by-doing, as modern endogenous growth theorists have postulated.

By around 1750 Britain had reached a stage where the market was large enough, in a number of industries, to encourage numerous individuals to undertake expensive inventive activity. Of course, there was no one precise date when this suddenly became possible. The Darbys had been conducting their experiments since the 1710s; Lewis and Paul embarked on their inventive career in the 1730s; Hargreaves and Arkwright started in the late 1750s or 1760s. But the process does seem to have accelerated around mid-century. An explanation of invention based on market size should be clearly distinguished from orthodox demand-side explanations which explain invention as in some way stimulated by a shift in demand curves – their inability to do this was discussed in Chapters 4 and 5. Market-size explanations do not assume continuously growing demand. The only assumption is that the market must have grown in the recent past to reach an appropriate size.

Market size was particularly significant for patentable inventions, and thus the existence of the patent system was of prime importance. The fact that the patent system existed and worked was, in part, a happy accident, given that it had originated for other purposes. The system can legitimately be criticised for being too expensive and roundabout, therefore adding substantially to the costs of invention. But to criticise it, as was frequently done at the time and subsequently, for allowing sole rights to inventors for too long, thereby yielding them excessive profit and delaying diffusion, is to miss the entire point. By guaranteeing that a successful inventor would profit, inventiveness was encouraged. It was better to have the inventions, even if their diffusion was delayed, than not to have them at all.

Important though patents were, there were many inventions which were either not patented by choice, or were very difficult to patent. Many were process-type improvements such as coke-smelting; in such cases the inventor could be reasonably sure, in the early days, of a substantial period before the complex tacit knowledge and skill embodied in the technique could be copied. In other words, for a period the first user would still be able to reap some superprofit. In many cases, such inventions were fostered by a process of learning-by-doing. This was particularly important in the coal and metallurgical industries because of Britain's long history of coal use; tacit knowledge and skill were important in coalmining and use, and these had been built up over many years.

Such knowledge and skill constituted forms of human capital, the third component of endogenous growth. (One could add knowledge capital, that is disembodied knowledge: in the early days, the tacit nature of most industrial knowledge meant that, to be useful, it was usually embodied in the form of human capital; in other words, since it was not written down in books it was only accessible via individuals, and so for the sake of simplicity we do not need to consider knowledge capital separately.) Knowledge of coal use was a form of human capital in which Britain did have a substantial advantage, and Britain had a greater density of skills in wood- and metal-working than France, which reduced the cost of developing new types of machinery and enhanced opportunities for microinvention. In knowledge of pure science, however, Britain was probably matched, or nearly matched, in several European countries.

If the development of a large home market was crucial, what lay behind this development? In part it was a function of population, since as long as this did not outrun the capacity of land or the existing rate of investment, the larger the population the larger the total demand. In the mid-eighteenth century Britain's population size was more or less optimum given existing capital resources and agricultural techniques. This can be inferred from the fact that, soon afterwards, real wages in southern England declined as population growth quickened. Britain's population in the mid-eighteenth century was almost four times that of Holland, and thus Britain had a considerable advantage over the country closest to it in the level of income per person.

Income per person was the second main variable, and the fact that this was relatively high in Britain was largely due to agricultural prosperity. By 1750 output per person employed in agriculture may have been almost twice the French level. This yielded a surplus to many agriculturalists, ranging from small to middling farmers who could afford the odd piece of earthenware, to the gentry who could rebuild their houses and take an annual trip to Bath, to the great landowners who could afford a London house and all its appurtenances as well as a mansion in the country. In turn, agriculturalists' demand for services and industrial products supported a network of flourishing towns whose middle class provided another large market for goods and services. Agriculture has not been discussed in this book, since its focus is upon industrial change, but change in agriculture – the 'Agricultural Revolution' beloved of school textbook writers – was of fundamental importance to early British industrialisation. Historians have pointed to the fact that agricultural demand for industrial goods was less than non-agricultural demand, but this is to miss the point that many non-agriculturalists, ranging from the carters who provided transport, to the shopkeepers of market towns, to the aristocratic families living in London but dependent on agricultural rents, ultimately owed their income to the prosperity of agriculture. There is still much debate among agricultural historians as to the exact timing of advances in techniques, but there is general agreement that British agriculture was already relatively advanced by the late seventeenth century, and continued to improve from then on. Many agricultural historians dislike the term 'Agricultural Revolution', because in reality change occurred over a long period and was ongoing.

It is difficult to separate out other components of Britain's mid-eighteenth-century prosperity. Many can be summarised in the phrase 'Smithian growth'. That is, the division of labour had advanced substantially and productivity had risen as a consequence. The benefits of Smithian growth increased in line with the size of the market, which brings us back to agriculture. But there were other factors which widened and integrated markets: these included export growth and good transport links. The latter had already been improved by small-scale capital investment, particularly in river navigations, but for the most part they were a gift of nature, comprising the sea and the already navigable rivers. One final cause of a larger market was the existing technical advance in industry. Since the late seventeenth century there had been a stream of new products, particularly in the textiles and pottery industries; there had also been important cost-reducing inventions, especially in industries such as glass and non-ferrous metal-smelting, where coal had already been substituted for wood. The early fall in the price of consumer goods noted in Chapter 4 suggests that these early inventions had a real impact and, by increasing prosperity, they increased market size. Smithian growth, therefore, was running side by side with, and to some extent dependent on, growth based on invention and innovation. Much of this was a consequence of learning-by-doing, particularly in coal-using industries. Britain's endowment of coal was therefore an asset not just because of the value of the mineral itself, but because its early use had allowed learning-by-doing effects to develop.

The argument, therefore, is that the British market reached a critical size in the mid-eighteenth century, such that the rewards to costly invention reached a level where it became worthwhile to devote substantial amounts of time and money to it. Once this critical market size had accelerated the inventive process, learning-by-doing effects also accelerated because, the more new inventions were in circulation, the more the opportunity for learning-by-doing to be applied to each one. The acceleration of invention did not downgrade other elements of growth, however. Crucially, invention and innovation raised the return to investment and thus its volume; so not only were there more new techniques, but they were installed at a faster rate. Autonomous export growth continued, as has already been noted. More important, Smithian growth also accelerated because faster growth in the industrial economy accelerated the growth in the total national market, leading to greater specialisation. Smithian growth was promoted by a particularly rapid reduction in transport costs, fostered by innovation and capital investment. This in turn opened up more profit opportunities, thus further stimulating investment, innovation and the improvement of X-efficiency: Smithian growth fostered Schumpeterian growth.

One final ingredient in the growth process was the further development of human capital, which for the most part took place as it always had done, as a by-product of work, but on a much larger scale as industry developed, and with greater efficiency as a result of specialisation. Rapid industrial growth meant that Britain continued to enjoy a higher level of industrial skills than other countries, concentrated in and around the industries which were already predominant: textiles, coal, iron, metalworking and chemicals. These skills fostered further macroinventions, especially in machine tools and in the application of the steam engine to railways (unless this is regarded as a super-microinvention). It also furthered Britain's capacity for microinvention. For instance, the continuous paper machine, although a French invention, was developed in Britain, largely through the skill of the engineer Bryan Donkin. But impressive though British practical skills were, by the end of the period there was underinvestment in formal education.

Smithian growth is one of the few models which does not fit into the two broad categories outlined earlier: those which focus on capital accumulation and those which focus on invention and innovation. (To take advantage of the division of labour does, of course, require changes in organisation; but in Smithian growth, while organisation would change, technology could remain static.) Smithian growth forms one half of another model which lies outside these two categories, that put forward by Tony Wrigley. Wrigley postulates a period of Smithian growth in Britain, followed by growth that was coal-fuelled. Therefore the factor of production on which Wrigley's model lays most emphasis is land, which other models neglect. To Wrigley, Smithian growth was important but it had limits set by the tendency to decreasing returns to land. Coal overcame these. Chronologically, of course, Smithian growth and coal-based growth overlapped, but analytically the model separates them. Invention is part of the model, although it is not prominent in Wrigley's exposition, since invention was necessary to develop coal-using techniques. Such invention could be explained partly as a result of learning-by-doing, as in the case of coke-smelting. Increasingly, however, coal-using techniques depended on costly, patentable inventions such as the steam engine and Cort's puddling furnace and rolling mills. Wrigley's separation of Smithian growth and coal-based growth is therefore questionable. The two were connected because market size was crucial both to Smithian growth and to the process of invention on which advances in coal use depended.

One can speculate that, without coal but with the market size reached in the mid-eighteenth century, there might still have been a period of inventiveness centred upon hand- and water-powered machinery, of which the jenny and the waterframe are classic examples. There might have been half an Industrial Revolution, and it would have been greener and less smoky than the one which actually happened. However, such environmentally-friendly speculation cannot be pushed too far. As time went by, coal and coal-using inventions became increasingly important and, as such, helped to maintain and increase national income. Therefore market size and its continued capacity to motivate inventors came to depend in part on coal use.

Although one can criticise Wrigley's analytical separation of Smithian growth from coal-based growth, and his downplaying of inventiveness, his model is of great importance because it helps to explain the continuation of the British Industrial Revolution in the face of diminishing returns due to population increase. If an endogenous process of invention must be accorded first place in the hierarchy of causation, coal is in second place due to its crucial role in maintaining the momentum of change.

In spite of the momentum provided by coal, growth was relatively slow compared with most subsequent industrialisers, from North America in the late nineteenth century to East Asia in the late twentieth. This was because innovation and productivity change, though fast in textiles, iron and the transport sector, were slow elsewhere. As a result, Britain developed an industrial economy which has been described as skewed, with a heavy concentration on the first two sectors and coal. But there can be no fair comparison between the British Industrial Revolution and later ones. Britain had enjoyed an extraordinary spate of macroinventions in the second half of the eighteenth century; because of this there was massive scope for microinventiveness and learning-by-doing improvements in the core industries over the next fifty to one hundred years. A further disincentive to inventive activity outside existing technologies was the relatively small market for most consumer goods because of the slow growth in living standards. Finally, there were practical limits, set by the supply of knowledge and skills, on how inventive the British could be. All these factors limited the supply of radically new technologies once the initial macroinventions had been made. Industrialisers in the nineteenth century – mainly European countries and America – had to overcome major hurdles, in part because British competition tended to force up the size at which entry to a market became viable. But in another way, their task was relatively easy because they could import technology, usually from Britain itself. The same principle has been true for all subsequent industrialising countries. In the British Industrial Revolution new technology had to be invented; it was not available off the shelf; and inventing was a laborious and expensive process.

Impacts

The Industrial Revolution was an economic phenomenon, but it is often associated with a type of society: one in which the majority of people lived in overcrowded urban areas, were overworked, sometimes unemployed, frequently ill and always the victims of inequality. Against that view are ranged more optimistic assessments: according to these, industrialisation gave people more choice of work, more opportunities for regular work, better wages, warmer houses and cheaper clothing; and if conditions in town and country were still poor in 1850, they were to become much better over the next fifty years.

To some extent both assessments are correct, for the assertions in them are not incompatible: people could suffer worse health, but still be warmer and better clothed. Equally important, the adverse trends were not, for the most part, the sole result of industrialisation. Industrialisation was a major reason for the problems of public health, because without it towns would have grown more slowly and been less crowded. But the rapid growth of population brought other problems which, without industrialisation, would have been far worse. The British population would have had less command over the food resources of Europe, because Britain would not have had the same ability to pay for them. The spectre of famine – the apogee of Malthusian crisis – was near at hand in Europe in the 1840s: Ireland's suffering was most acute and there were special reasons for that, but Scandinavian countries too came very close to crisis. In older historiography, the 1840s in Britain were the 'Hungry Forties'. It was a miserable period for many, with urban health problems and rural unemployment at their worst, and a severe cyclical depression at the beginning of the decade. But people in Britain did not die from sheer want of food. If the Industrial Revolution had not taken place, the Hungry Forties would almost certainly have been a reality and not just a half-forgotten myth.

To take 1850 as a turning point, and a neat terminal date for this book, is in one sense merely a convenience. But it is as apposite a date as any other. Increasingly from the mid-century, the transport improvements which industrialisation had made possible eased the food supply situation by making it economically feasible for new land to be used to supply European economies. Cities started to be cleaned up, although very slowly at first. And railways, again very slowly, facilitated some dispersal of industry and services in the south and encouraged a gradual widening of employment opportunities. The positive effects of the Industrial Revolution had always been there but for a long time they were obscured by a host of other problems, some caused by industrialisation but most not. From 1850 on the positive effects became increasingly visible.

Whether its social impact was negative or positive, the economic impact of the Industrial Revolution seems undisputed. Britain in 1850 was an economic colossus, a position which it held virtually unchallenged until around 1870, when it provided over 40 per cent of world exports of manufactured goods. From then on, its position in the world economy was slowly eroded as Continental countries and the United States industrialised. In absolute terms the British economy still grew rapidly – this was partly why living standards increased – but in relative terms Britain suffered an apparently inexorable economic decline which may or may not have come to an end at the present day. This is a process which seems disconnected from the heroic achievements of the Industrial Revolution; some economic historians, however, always eager to find the worm in the bud, see decline as rooted in precisely those achievements.

The pessimistic account of the economic achievements of the Industrial Revolution can be summarised as follows. From around 1850 Britain's skewed industrialisation set it on a low-growth path for two reasons: the very heavy orientation towards textiles provided Britain with an industry which continued to grow but at a much slower rate than previously, as countries with lower wages competed successfully; and with this there was a lack of human capital endowment.

If 1850 is taken as a benchmark, the orientation towards textiles is true, although whether or not it necessarily slowed Britain's future economic progress is questionable. Britain had a huge textile industry, but there is no reason to think that this locked the country irrevocably into a particular industrial structure. It is often forgotten that Japan, now one of the most technologically advanced economies in the world, recovered in the 1950s from war on the back of its textile industry. That was followed in the 1960s by a turn to basic metal industries – steel and shipbuilding. It was only in the 1970s that its strengths in the production of cars and electronic goods were established. This brief analogy suggests that individual industries, however important, do not dictate a country's industrial path. Rapid innovation will generate a high rate of investment in new industries, and that by itself will shift industrial structures. In turn, this investment will lift wage levels. Old industries find themselves unable to compete with cheap labour countries and wither away, to be replaced by the new.

Human capital endowments in Britain suffered from the

indifferent quality of formal education, but in spite of that it is highly unlikely that Britain was worse off *in toto* than most Continental economies. In formal educational qualifications as measured by literacy, Britain by the mid-nineteenth century was on a par with France and Belgium – the next most industrialised countries after Britain – although worse off than Germany, Holland and the Scandinavian countries. But in industrial work skills Britain must still have been greatly superior, as most practical skills in Continental Europe were still artisan-based: sometimes relevant to large-scale industry, as in the case of smiths and other metal workers, but often not.

So the state of Britain in 1850 does not provide an answer, although it may provide clues, as to why invention and innovation slowed down relative to other countries. Increasingly after 1850, as technology developed further, the on-the-job training which was adequate during the Industrial Revolution and up to the mid-nineteenth century became only part of the solution to the problem of developing skills. Advanced skills became more and more important, not just to the process of invention and innovation but also to understanding why innovations were important and how new machinery could best be utilised on the factory floor. Basic industrial skills in Britain probably remained adequate until well into the twentieth century. But – and this is a familiar thesis – Britain did fall behind in the supply of more advanced skills: those, for instance, of the electrical engineer, the chemist and the production manager. This is often linked with the poor quality of formal education, both at a basic and at a higher level. Yet in economic terms, it would have been perfectly possible for later nineteenth-century Britain to have invested heavily in schools, polytechnics and so forth if Parliament and people had wished, because Britain was a very rich country by most standards. To some extent this was done, but it was not done as much as elsewhere for complex societal reasons. The Industrial Revolution helped to bring about that society and so is in some sense implicated, but many other factors had made the type of society and government Britain had in the nineteenth and twentieth centuries. Therefore to posit rigid links between the industrial structure bequeathed by the Industrial Revolution down to 1850, and Britain's subsequent economic development, is to oversimplify. Human agency could have altered the path of development; but much of the time it chose not to.

Envoi

The model of the British Industrial Revolution sketched here is of endogenous growth in which three components came together: sufficient human capital; a market large enough to stimulate invention; and a patent system allowing the rewards of invention to be captured. Human capital was already leading to learning-by-doing type invention in coal-using industries; human capital, market size and the patent system together stimulated invention in machinery, particularly textile machinery, but also the steam engine. Once a cluster of inventions had occurred, learning-by-doing effects accelerated and market size grew further, because of rising national income which was due in part to previous invention. So, with the help of coal, the Industrial Revolution became self-perpetuating although it was limited in scope for a long period.

These causal factors could not have existed without previous stimuli. Here Rostow's concept of preconditions, that is, conditions which are necessary for industrialisation to take place but are not by themselves sufficient, is helpful. It has often been criticised on the grounds that it is tautological: an industrial revolution cannot occur on a desert island; there must, at least, be capital and labour in some form as well as land. But although this is true, we can be more precise about the preconditions in Britain and this gives the concept utility. For market size, the necessary preconditions in the context of the eighteenth century were productive agriculture, reasonable transport and a fair-sized national polity. For human capital, the preconditions were primarily those factors which encouraged Britain's industrial development, and therefore the accumulation of practical skills, before the Industrial Revolution proper: in particular easily accessible coal, and a large enough demand for goods such as glass and copper whose production techniques were susceptible to improvement – thus taking us back to market size. The main precondition for a workable patent system was a degree of luck – luck that a system designed for one purpose was workable for another. Both the proximate causes and the important preconditions suggest that the Industrial Revolution was not likely to have occurred elsewhere at the time it did in Britain. The Dutch market was much smaller, and it is a striking fact that Dutch industrial patents fell to their lowest level for over a century in 1750, just as British patents began their rapid increase. The

French market was limited by the poverty of its agriculture and poor transport. Both countries lacked easily accessible coal and the human capital developed by the early growth of coal-using technology.

However, it flies in the face of common sense to suggest that we would still be living in a pre-industrial world if Britain in 1750 had been a bit poorer than it was, or its coal seams a few hundred feet deeper. Europe had seen a number of major industrial innovations in the previous few hundred years; agricultural techniques had advanced in other countries besides Britain; the frontiers of the European-dominated world had been pushed steadily outwards; huge scientific advances had taken place. Surely in these circumstances industrial change would have taken place sooner rather than later? Almost certainly it would have done, because industrial revolutions do not have to take a particular form. Britain's route was one of several possibilities. Invention could have taken place outside the market framework, as it often did in Britain: learning-by-doing was one source – and Britain was not the only country with coal, the use of which provided a major source of learning-by-doing type inventions; or scientific advance, relatively unimportant in Britain, could have fostered invention. Market size in much of Europe may have been too small to encourage profit-related invention, but in North America ample land was already creating a wealthy population which was coming to constitute a major market in its own right.

So in a sense the British Industrial Revolution was, as historians of longer-term change like to point out, only a part of a wider process of European economic expansion. The timing and course of the Revolution were unique, however: without it Britain would have been very different. The poverty experienced by rural labourers in the south would have been endemic over the whole country, although there would have been fewer urban slums with their associated disease and mortality. The government would have been poorer too, and its ability to command foreign exchange would have been reduced. Deprived of the wherewithal to bribe Continental allies, it is far from certain that Britain would have beaten Napoleon. The plump, opulent John Bull of the mid-eighteenth century would have grown lean and haggard; out of the fog of counterfactual speculation looms a poor, overpopulated and perhaps defeated island.

Further reading

For the prosperity of agriculture R.C. Allen, 'Tracking' and M. Overton, *Agricultural Revolution* (see Chapter 7), although they disagree about the timing of change; for a long-term and comparative view P.K. O'Brien, 'Path dependency: or why Britain became an industrialised and urbanised economy long before France', *EcHR*, 49 (1996), pp. 213–49; there is a thought-provoking perspective on this in P.M. Solar, 'English poor relief' (see Chapter 3). For skewed growth N.F.R. Crafts, *British Economic Growth* (see Introduction); Crafts points out that post-1850 human capital formation could have been improved if the will had been there. For the context of long-term growth in Europe W.W. Rostow, *How it All Began: Origins of the Modern Economy* (1975); E.L. Jones, *European Miracle* (see chapter 4); G.D. Snooks, *Was the Industrial Revolution Necessary?* (1994). M. Sanderson, *Education and Economic Decline in Britain 1870 to the 1990s* (Cambridge, 1999) is very useful for education after the Industrial Revolution; it takes a rather more sanguine view of the late Victorian and Edwardian period than the one expressed in this book.

Measuring growth

Over the last twenty years a sharp revision has taken place in generally accepted views of the rate of economic growth during the British
Industrial Revolution. In the 1960s the publication of figures compiled by Phyllis Deane and Max Cole suggested that output grew
quite rapidly from the 1780s onwards. More recently, however,
Nick Crafts and Knick Harley have suggested substantial revisions
of the figures which indicate a much lower growth rate. Their main
differences from Deane and Cole lie in their estimates of manufacturing and mining output, which they believe was much higher in
the early and mid-eighteenth century than had hitherto been
thought. Thus whereas Deane and Cole find industrial production
increasing almost sixfold between 1780 and 1830, Crafts and
Harley think it increased by less than four times. Their view has
been criticised by a number of scholars, although most of the criticisms have been partial rather than comprehensive. Crafts and
Harley have adjusted their original figures but still hold to their original conception of slow growth. Some of the criticisms may well
have some validity and will be discussed later in the Appendix. But
most, even if accepted, would not make a substantial difference to
the Crafts–Harley scenario. Furthermore there are two arguments in
favour of the slow-growth scenario.

The first argument is qualitative. Britain in the first half of the
eighteenth century was, by international standards, a prosperous
economy: no large group in the population was short of food;
consumer goods were spreading rapidly; expenditure on poor relief
was low; agriculture probably accounted for less than 40 per cent
of national income – a smaller proportion than Germany in the
mid-nineteenth or Russia in the early twentieth centuries; and

concomitantly, industry was quite important. By around 1830 there were enormous changes in the economy: canals had been built and railways were being built; cotton and iron production had been revolutionised and machinery production was now a major industry. However, the changes need to be put in perspective. Agriculture still accounted for around one quarter of national income, while about 15 per cent of the workforce were in domestic service and could not have contributed measurably to economic growth. Many people were still very poor: the Swing riots, a great rural protest movement ostensibly directed against machinery but stimulated by the labourers' poverty, took place throughout southern England in 1830–31; large groups of industrial workers, particularly textile workers in the south and west, were likewise suffering severe deprivation. So economic advance was mixed with economic retardation and widespread poverty. In the light of this, Deane's and Cole's statistics, which suggest that average incomes per person had doubled over the period 1780 to 1830, are hard to accept.

Charles Feinstein's recent calculations of real wages, discussed in Chapter 7, provide quantitative support for the Crafts–Harley view. Feinstein's figures are derived from money wages and prices, making them largely independent of Crafts' and Harley's, which are estimates of output. Broadly speaking, wages are likely to increase at a similar rate to income per person, although there will be some divergences. So real wage figures provide some check on income per person and hence on national income.

The wage figures are not likely to exactly parallel income-per-person figures for various reasons. The latter are an arithmetical construct, obtained by dividing estimates of national income by population: therefore they incorporate those parts of national income going to investment, which rose over the period, and to government expenditure, which rose during the wars and then fell; in addition, they take no account of fluctuations in the share of income going to particular groups in the period, whereas real wages would reflect a fall or rise in the share going to wage-earners. Even if the share changed, however, it would not have been likely to lead to massive differences in real wages as compared with incomes per person. Finally, real wages were subject to quite substantial fluctuations due to the impact of booms and depressions; ideally national income figures would also reflect these, but the broad figures we have do not do so. The resemblance between the two sets of figures in Table A.1 at different dates is therefore extremely interesting and suggestive, but should not be taken to mean that either figure, at any one date, is a precise snapshot of the true state of affairs. The resemblance is further strengthened because part of the discrepancy for 1801 and 1831 can be accounted for by the rise in the investment ratio: this would depress the rise in real wages since, if more national income went to investment, less would be available for wages. The growing discrepancy in later years is odd, since it is usually assumed that output figures after 1830 are more reliable than before, but it is not our concern. From our point of view the significant point is that the wage figures support the finding that there was only a slow growth of income per person in the period 1780–1831. Since, as stated, the income-per-person figures derive directly from the national income figures, the slow growth of real wages provides very strong support for believing that national income also grew slowly.

The assumed figures for increases in national income generate estimates for changes in total factor productivity (TFP). The concept of TFP is reasonably simple. National income – or output, which comes to the same thing – is the end product of the combination of the three factors of production: land, labour and capital. If the increase in output growth is greater than the increase in these inputs, then there must be additional growth coming from somewhere – technical and organisational change, for example. This additional growth is sometimes known as the residual, since it is the residue left after subtracting the contribution of the other factors. TFP is a more dignified name for the same thing, justified because when the contribution of measurable inputs is stripped out, any further increase must be due to productivity change of one kind or another. Its calculation is not difficult since, apart from national output growth itself, the only figures needed are estimates of the share of land, labour and capital in the productive process and of changes in these factors. However, given the uncertainties attaching in our period to output growth, as well as the difficulty of accurately estimating shares, any figures produced for TFP growth are obviously problematic.

Before discussing the level of TFP growth in the period, three features associated with the concept need to be addressed. The first relates to technical problems of calculation. The economic theory which justifies the estimation of TFP growth assumes constant returns to scale; in practice, when the growth rate is small, the scope for increasing returns is limited and it is unlikely to significantly affect calculated TFP growth. Theory also assumes that each factor's income is commensurate with its marginal product – that is, increments in output will be exactly reflected in increments in income. However, even though supernormal profits were likely in some industries, these contributed only a small share of national income and would not make much difference to TFP calculations for our period.

The second problem relates to the causation of TFP increases. Many would argue that improvements in human capital are an important component of such increases, and to that extent the residual, in part, records an inability to properly measure such improvements. However, as Chapter 3 suggests, the Industrial Revolution period was unlikely to have seen large improvements in human capital in relation to output growth: capital accumulation through on-the-job training may have increased, but such increases could have been partially offset by the lack of any significant improvement in basic education; almost certainly the productivity of training increased because of the division of labour, but again there is no quantification. Apart from human capital improvements, the other crucial component of TFP increase was invention, both of technology and organisation, which was manifested in innovation. Invention could be regarded as knowledge capital, although again quantification seems virtually impossible or, at any rate, has not been attempted. And beneficial externalities and increasing returns, in practice, even if frowned upon in theory, cannot be discounted as unenumerated sources of residual economic growth.

The third and most important feature of TFP is that its enumeration does not imply causation. In other words, to estimate TFP's percentage contribution to economic growth does not imply that technical and organisational change made just that contribution and no other. The argument developed in this book is that invention was central because it raised profit rates: capital accumulation and an increase in labour input followed. Therefore the equation which shows the shares of capital, labour, land and TFP in economic growth does not demonstrate a functional relationship between each of those things and growth: it is an accounting identity. By enumerating the proximate contributions of each to growth it clarifies aspects of the growth process, but it does not tell us why that process occurred.

Bearing in mind those caveats, what do the output figures tell us about changes in TFP? If Crafts' and Harley's figures are accepted, output grew slowly during the Industrial Revolution, and so as a matter of arithmetical calculation TFP must also have grown slowly given that capital and labour were increasing. Crafts and Harley estimate average TFP growth in Britain to be 0.55 per cent per annum between 1780 and 1860 – small by the standards of the twentieth century. Furthermore, they think that around one-third of this arose from agricultural improvement, leaving only two-thirds to come from productivity growth in manufacturing and other modernised sectors such as railways, canals and shipping. Disaggregating TFP growth into sectors, they suggest that there was practically no growth in manufacturing outside textiles and iron, or in services besides the transport modes mentioned above. A number of scholars, notably Maxine Berg, Pat Hudson and Peter Temin, have taken issue with this, pointing out how widespread technical change and the division of labour were outside these sectors; their arguments are intuitively plausible if, so far, lacking quantification. However, as has been seen, it is difficult to see how Crafts' and Harley's underlying figures can be fundamentally wrong, given the support they gain from wage estimates. Is it possible to find some common ground between such apparently irreconcilable positions?

Even small adjustments to the Crafts–Harley input or output figures could make a significant difference to the residual, so it is worth seeing whether such adjustments might reasonably be made. It is possible that the factor input figures are incorrect, but the capital figures do utilise the best information available and at present there are no evidential or conceptual grounds for questioning them. The labour force figures are more problematic; it is frequently conjectured that hours of work per person increased; there are similar uncertainties about the amount of women's and children's paid work, since it has been argued that this was underrecorded in the census which began in 1801. However, an increase in hours or in labour participation would result in an increase in total labour input and therefore a decrease in the rate of TFP growth. In truth, our knowledge of these issues is still uncertain enough to make it quite possible that there was a decline in hours worked or female/child participation, thus pushing up the TFP growth rate, although probably not by much.

However, since knowledge is uncertain, any such conclusion is purely speculative.

Criticism of the figures for output/national income runs into the problem that real wages apparently rose more slowly than income per person, suggesting that the latter is too high and, again, that TFP growth might actually be overestimated. There were factors which could account for the differential. Cyclical unemployment depressed wages in particular years: the years immediately after 1801 and 1831 saw quite a sharp rise in real wages, although not enough to completely close the gap in Table A.1. As suggested in Chapter 7, it may be that relative price changes in the period 1780–1830 also tended to depress real wages and, conversely, to advantage those with higher incomes, thus closing the gap still further. So the apparent gap between real incomes and wages might still be closed and even allow us to postulate some increase in the Crafts–Harley income figures. However, the low level of real-wage growth strongly suggests that their income figures cannot be significantly understated; and when we get to the period 1830–70 we find a much larger real-wage/income per person gap opening up, which is harder to reconcile. So if the figures for growth of income are roughly correct, and if subsequent reworking is unlikely to increase them much, it remains difficult to argue that the figure of 0.55 per cent per annum for TFP growth, which relates to the whole period 1780–1860, is too low.

It might be better to assume that 0.55 per cent is broadly correct and then to explain why such low TFP growth is compatible with the innovation we know occurred. Crafts' and Harley's own explanation is straightforward. Large areas of the economy remained virtually unaffected by either technical or organisational change: these included traditional trades such as tailoring, seamstressing, boot- and shoe-making and building; retail trade, although here there may have been uncounted quality changes as shops became larger, better stocked and better lit; laundrywork and domestic service. Even with innovation in some parts of the economy, these areas and others acted as deadweights, reducing the total increase. A more radical approach, but along similar lines, would be to suggest that productivity might have actually declined in some sectors of the economy. The rapid increase in population may have led to an increase, first in agricultural and then in urban underemployment, the latter manifesting itself as the casual labour to which so many mid-Victorian observers drew attention. Strictly speaking, this would constitute a reduction in hours worked; but if each worker was counted as full-time then statistically it would appear as a fall in labour productivity, and hence of TFP. To counterbalance this there would have to be a larger TFP increase in sectors which did not employ many casual workers, which included the modernising manufacturing sectors. Therefore TFP in these sectors – which as well as textiles and iron would include machinery construction, paper-making and other industries – could have grown by rather more than Crafts and Harley suggest. This would provide a partial reconciliation between their views and those of their critics.

However one cuts up the figures, it seems likely that the broad picture of slow growth, by modern standards, is correct. But relatively slow growth is still compatible over a period of fifty to a hundred years with massive structural change. Nor does an acceptance of slow growth preclude a belief that the changes which did occur were a complete break with the past – that is, that they were revolutionary.

Table

Table A.1 Income per person and real wages

	Income per person	Real wages	
1780	100	100	(1788–82)
1801	108	103	(1798–1802)
1831	125	111	(1828–32)
1870	225	149	(1868–72)

Sources: Income per person from Harley, 'Reassessing the Industrial Revolution', p. 194 (see Chapter 2); real wages from Feinstein, 'Pessimism perpetuated' (see Chapter 7)

Further reading

M. Berg and P. Hudson, 'Rehabilitating the industrial revolution', *EcHR*, 45 (1992), pp. 24–50.

N.F.R. Crafts, *British Economic Growth* (see Introduction).

N.F.R. Crafts and C.K. Harley, 'Output growth and the British industrial revolution: a restatement of the Crafts–Harley view', *EcHR*, 45 (1992), pp. 703–30.

N.F.R. Crafts and T.C. Mills, 'The industrial revolution as a macroeconomic epoch: an alternative view', *EcHR*, 47 (1994), pp. 769–75.

P. Deane and W.A. Cole, *British Economic Growth 1688–1959* (Cambridge 1967).

C.H. Feinstein, 'Pessimism perpetuated' (see Chapter 7).

D. Greasley and L. Oxley, 'Rehabilitation sustained: the industrial revolution as a macroeconomic epoch', *EcHR*, 47 (1994), pp. 760–8.

C.K. Harley, 'Reassessing the industrial revolution' (see Chapter 2).

C.K. Harley and N.F.R. Crafts, 'Productivity growth during the first industrial revolution: inferences from the pattern of British external trade', *LSE Working Papers in Economic History*, 42/98 (1998).

R.V. Jackson, 'Rates of industrial growth during the industrial revolution', *EcHR*, 45 (1992), pp. 1–23.

P. Temin, 'Two views of the British industrial revolution', *JEH*, 57 (1997), pp. 1–33.

Index